*Hartshorne and the Metaphysics
of Animal Rights*

SUNY Series in Philosophy

Robert Cummings Neville, Editor

Hartshorne
and the
Metaphysics
of Animal Rights

Daniel A. Dombrowski

State University of New York Press

Published by
State University of New York Press, Albany

© 1988   State University of New York

For information, address State University of New York
Press, State University Plaza, Albany, N.Y. 12246

Library of Congress Cataloging in Publication Data
Dombrowski, Daniel A.
    Hartshorne and the metaphysics of animal rights / Daniel A. Dombrowski
        p.   cm. — (SUNY series in philosophy)
    Bibliography: p. 152
    Includes index.
    ISBN 0-88706-704-2.   ISBN 0-88706-705-0 (pbk.)
    1. Hartshorne, Charles, 1897-   . 2. God. 3. Animals
4. Vegetarianism. 5. Metaphysics. I. Title. II. Series.
B945.H354D65 1988
179′ .3—dc19   87-16591
                                                                       CIP

To Kathie

Contents

Abbreviations of Works
by Charles Hartshorne

Introduction

In an earlier book, *The Philosophy of Vegetarianism*, I tried to provide what I saw as some much-needed historical depth to recent debates on animal rights and environmental ethics. The book's title could have been better chosen, as a reviewer in *Ethics* noted, since its primary focus was ancient Greek philosophy, specifically the thinkers in antiquity who were vegetarian or anti-vegetarian. The present book, although it is self-contained and does not pre-suppose a reading of the first book, is continuous with *The Philosophy of Vegetarianism*[1] in two ways.

First, in that the vegetarian tradition in antiquity travelled along the Pythagorean–Platonic–Neoplatonic axis, it is important to note that Charles Hartshorne, when he boasts that "I have always been something of a Platonist" (EA; 164-165[2]), correctly places himself along the same axis. Indeed, the present volume is *primarily* about the relationship between Hartshorne's theory of God and his thoughts on animals. But as I will argue in Chapter Seven, this relationship only makes sense against the background of Hartshorne's Platonism, which has received far too little attention from scholars. It is my hope that exploring Hartshorne's thought on God, animals, Plato, and neoplatonizing romanticism (see Chapter Six) does not constitute four separate endeavors. Rather, by showing how Hartshorne's thought is woven out of these four threads I hope to make a contribution to understanding his philosophy.

Almost all of the enormous attention his work has received has been on his dipolar theism or on his defense of St. Anselm's ontological argument, and rightfully so. Nonetheless, Hartshorne has written extensively on animals, both as a philosopher of nature and as an expert on bird song. Especially since his magnum opus appeared in 1970, *Creative Synthesis and Philosophic Method* (CS), he has devoted a great deal of attention to animals, and for several reasons that will be treated in this book. Not the least of these is that a treatment of the relationship between human beings and animals helps us to better understand our relationship with God.

1

Second, whereas *The Philosophy of Vegetarianism* was an attempt to add historical depth to certain contemporary debates in philosophy regarding animals, the present book is an attempt to expand the contemporary debates themselves by providing them greater metaphysical depth. That is, in addition to being a book about Hartshorne it is *secondarily* an attempt to use Hartshorne to defend philosophic vegetarianism. Although this is not exactly Hartshorne's own view, he does at several points, as we shall see, indicate the strengths he sees in the vegetarian position. I will suggest that, given what Hartshorne says about God, animals, plants, and ethics, we should be attracted to vegetarianism. Quite appropriately (I have Mrs. Dorothy Hartshorne to thank for this information), the etymological root of Hartshorne's own name means "deer's refuge."

Both in my explication of Hartshorne's views of God and animals and in my use of Hartshorne to defend philosophic vegetarianism, my own originality (or idiosyncracy) is evident, especially in the defense of the vegetarian position. I hope that whatever distinctiveness my argument has helps show the wisdom and efficacy of constructing a general philosophy of nature, indeed a metaphysics. Very soon after the rebirth of philosophic vegetarianism in the 1970s, initiated by philosophers such as Peter Singer and Tom Regan, came a realization that contracting the philosophical vision so as to see animals on their own terms was at once very fruitful and very frustrating. The frustration arose from an inability to determine the weight to be placed on the interests of animals when compared to possible values to be found in plants, bodies of water, and the land, not to mention the possible values to be found in future animals and other natural beings. Hence the growth of the somewhat more synoptic vision provided by a consideration of issues in environmental ethics as a whole, as opposed to animal rights alone.

But if there is a God, a *truly* synoptic vision is needed, or at least as wide a vision as is humanly possible, in order to weigh the values that any contingent being (humans, animals, plants, etc.) would have in comparison with a necessary existent (God). This is why metaphysics is needed in order to adequately treat philosophical issues regarding animals. Linguistic analysis has been invaluable in the past decade in the effort to isolate some key questions regarding animals (for example, what does it mean to say that animals have interests?). But other questions (for example, those dealing with the place of animals in the overall pattern[s] of the cosmos) can only be properly asked, and responded to, against the background of a coherent, rationally defensible theory regarding what must necessarily be the case for *any* animal as opposed to what is the case only contingently. That is, such a theory presupposes a metaphysics.

In the first volume of Arnold Toynbee's *A Study of History*, the author brilliantly shows how specialization within modern industrialized (or we might add, post-industrial) systems and the atomization of experience in the sciences have affected the work of most contemporary historians. Although some metaphysicians have bemoaned a similar phenomenon (that is, a distaste for synthesis) in philosophy, not many have noticed that the need for metaphysics becomes insistent when ecology emerges as an important consideration. Metaphysics is already implicit in ecology: a *logos* (rational understanding) of the *oikos* (the cosmos viewed as one household) presupposes, to say the least, a wide-angle view of reality. The widest possible viewpoint is provided by a metaphysical theory of what is necessary and what is contingent in reality.

These remarks should indicate how I would respond to the question, "Why study metaphysics in order to decide how to think about and treat animals?" But an added remark is needed to respond to the question, "Why a process metaphysics?" The explanatory role of "entities" in science (for example, as treated later, botanists explain growth in plants through cells, not nervous systems) should play a crucial role in determining what is metaphysically individual and what is metaphysically composite. Many contemporary philosophers would agree that an acceptable metaphysics must be compatible with the best available science. Because of this agreement, it is important to notice that process metaphysics came about as an improved empiricism, in the widest sense of that term. Alfred North Whitehead's thought combined Plato, Leibniz, and relativity physics. Whereas philosophers in the wake of Newtonian physics had postulated impenetrable, dead particles as ultimate, process metaphysics, in the wake of twentieth-century physics and Darwinian thought, favors fields of force and moments of experience as ultimate.

Because a unified world view consonant with contemporary science is a more plausible goal in process metaphysics that in its most prominent metaphysical competitors, process metaphysics is to be recommended. Heidegger has little to offer in terms of a world view consonant with science; in fact, he often exhibits an anti-scientific animus. And analytic theism, if indeed it is a metaphysics and not a philosophy of language, either is antithetical to the notion of a world view or leaves its ecology, in the widest sense of the term, only implicit. It is not at all clear how incredibly clever arguments of analytic theism in defense of divine omniscience or fideism can help us better understand or more justly treat animals. As we shall see, the notions in process thought of perspective and experience do provide us with depth of understanding and the moral reasons for better treatment of animals.

Finally, it may be asked, "Why Hartshorne?" The most obvious response is that, whereas analytic philosophers consider Alvin Plantinga as the premier living metaphysician or philosopher of religion, and those interested in continental philosophy may look to Paul Ricoeur, neither of these thinkers has devoted any attention to animals. In fact, in Plantinga's case, at least, it is unclear how his contemporary version of Augustinianism-Calvinism could say much that has not already been said from those perspectives about animals.[3] Hartshorne has not only had a great deal to say about animals, but he has also provided a still-neglected way out of disputes between the defenders of animal rights, who see individual animals as the prime loci of value in nature, and those concerned with environmental ethics, who see species or ecosystems as the prime loci of value.

By extending the concept of low-grade sentience or feeling through the whole world, Hartshorne allows that plants, rocks, and the earth all have value. What is unique about Hartshorne's thought, I think, is that he can extend value throughout creation yet still maintain the requirement that moral patients must be conscious. The former point preserves what is best in environmental ethics, whereas the latter point adds support to the case for animal rights, including philosophic vegetarianism. As I will argue, philosophic vegetarianism is an important issue because more than any other it focuses on the question of whether or not individual animals deserve our respect, and if so, how much. This is not to deny that at times the interests of individual animals must be balanced against the claims of human beings or of ecosystems, but deciding whether or not we will unnecessarily (from the perspective of bodily health) eat animals on a regular basis is already to resolve, at least implicitly, all of the major questions as to how we should view animals and how we should view their relationship to God.

The chapters of this book are arranged in a logical order. Chapter One offers a brief history of how animals have been viewed in a number of the world's great religions: Judaism, Christianity, Islam, Hinduism, Jainism, Buddhism, and Confucianism. I do not intend any exhaustive analysis of these traditions, not even of Judaism and Christianity, which receive the most attention. Rather, I hope to point up the dominant anthropocentrism, the human-centered views, of many great religions, including Christianity, so that their views on animals will provide a backdrop for Hartshorne's more sympathetic account. Chapter Two treats in detail Hartshorne's dipolar view of God, a treatment that is essential for seeing how Hartshorne's theories can improve on the theories of God and of animals that lie behind the world's great religions.

After these two preliminary chapters are three chapters that detail the nuances of Hartshorne's own thought on animals. Chapter Three treats the features that human beings share with animals, whereas Chapter Four treats those features that indicate that for Hartshorne human beings are superior to animals. That is, Chapters Three and Four outline a theory of unity-in-difference whereby Hartshorne does justice both to the post-Darwin commonplace that human beings are animals as well as to the traditional religious insight that there is something distinctive, something transcendent, about human beings. Chapter Five is an attempt to apply Hartshorne's theories regarding God and animals to some rather concrete practical concerns in ethics. It is in this chapter, more than any other, that I will be using Hartshorne to defend philosophic vegetarianism rather than trying to understand Hartshorne.

Chapters Six and Seven are attempts to ask the question, "What historical predecessors were there in the West for Hartshorne's view of God, which is so congenial to understanding and fair treatment of animals?" Whereas some would assume that Hartshorne's debt to Buddhism would have to bear most of the burden in the attempt to support his view of animals, I claim in Chapter Six that behind Hartshorne's views of God and animals is a highly reflective romanticism. (I should note that the lines of poetry at the beginning of each chapter are from William Wordsworth, whom both Hartshorne and Whitehead admire.) But if it is true that Wordsworth stands back of Hartshorne's views of God and animals, it is equally true that behind Wordsworth is Plato, whom Hartshorne is equally fond of using for his own purposes. It is in Chapter Seven, therefore, that the strongest link can be found between my earlier *The Philosophy of Vegetarianism* and the present book.

The upshot of Chapters Six and Seven is that whereas the dominant tune heard in Western culture regarding animals is either a cacophony or else a military march to accompany the wanton slaughter of animals for food, clothing, et al.—and this often enough in the name of religion—there is also a counterpoint sung by Plato, some of the romantic poets, and Hartshorne. It is difficult to hear this, however, because of the insistency of the dominant theme, which drowns out the counterpoint. This book is an attempt to turn the volume up on a theory of God and animals hardly heard at all in Judaism, Christianity, and Islam, and not heard loudly enough, surprisingly, in some Eastern religions.

I am aware of the fact that hearing things differently requires new aesthetic sensibilities. Hence in Chapter Eight I try to show that Hartshorne's aesthetics of bird song helps us better understand how considerations of God and animals mutually reinforce each other. I end with a brief Conclusion, where

I speculate as to what the saintly life of virtue would be like in our relations with animals. In this book I try to make Hartshorne's difficult texts intelligible in what I hope is clear English. I hope not only to accomplish my two aims, stated above, but also to highlight the tradition of St. Francis of Assisi, Teilhard de Chardin, and Hartshorne in Christian reflection on all of God's creation, not just human beings. Hartshorne's Franciscan roots will become apparent, and he has personally acknowledged his sympathy for Teilhard (CS; xv).

I should make it clear that my treatment of Hartshorne's thought will explain how his metaphysics helps us understand why animals deserve our respect. I will not offer a general theory of rights, which is obviously an enormous task, and a task already well performed by others, for example, Tom Regan. Rather, I will assume that human beings have rights and then show how Hartshorne's metaphysics forces us to take animal rights seriously.

Chapter One

A Brief History

The tendency, too potent in itself,
Of use and custom to bow down the soul
Under a growing weight of vulgar sense,
And substitute a universe of death
For that which moves with light and life informed,
Actual, divine, and true . . .
The mind condemned, without reprieve, to go
O'er life's long deserts with its charge of woe,
With sad congratulation joins the train
Where beasts and men together o'er the plain
Move on—a mighty caravan of pain.

The purpose of this chapter is to provide a standard against which I will later judge Hartshorne's theories of God and animals. The standard will be, in many respects, an easy one to raise, not because my reading of the history of religion is tendentious, but because most of the world's great religions have expected too little of themselves regarding animals. There is some reason to hope, however, that animals could receive their theological due in all of the religions I will treat.

Genesis 1:24–28 tells us that God made humans in God's divine image. Yet one might wonder whether human beings, who like to eat animals, also create God in their human image. Because human beings are said to be made in God's image, and nonhuman animals are not, humanity is given dominion over every living thing. This dominion includes killing and eating animals. After the Fall, God personally clothed Adam and Eve in animal skins (Genesis 3:21), thus we should not be surprised that human beings offered God animal sacrifices in return for God's goodness.[1] This reciprocation, naturally enough, put the fear of God and of human beings into animals (Genesis 9:1–3). It is true that human beings were given some guidance regarding animals. For example, they were not to boil a kid in its mother's milk (Exodus 23:19). But this offered no solace to the kid, who presumably could be boiled nonetheless. In fact, many laws regarding animals had nothing to do with animals per se, but rather with a condemnation of "pagan" (for example, Ugaritic) practices. It is also true that Isaiah predicted a time when the lion would lie down with the lamb. Unfortunately, there is no clear indication that the lamb could dwell peacefully with human beings. In short, for the Hebrews, human beings (or better, men) are the crown of creation, a status that denigrates animals.[2]

Asses and oxen were valuable as property, however. Perhaps this is why Jesus allows us to pull an animal out of a pit, even on a Sabbath (Luke 14:5). In general, the New Testament seems to leave animals in the same situation as in the Old. Jesus himself showed indifference (if not cruelty) to animals when he is portrayed by the gospel writer as having unnecessarily forced two thousand swine to hurl themselves into the sea (Matthew 5:1–13). St. Paul asked with scorn: Does God care for oxen? Of course not! (I Corinthians 9:9–10).

The example given by Jesus was not lost on later Christians. St. Augustine thought that to refrain from the killing of animals was the height of superstition, and that we need not behave toward animals with care.[3] Neither we nor God need care about animals. The kid that is not to be boiled in its mother's milk became a symbol for Christ.[4] Symbols, property, inferior pieces of creation meant for human beings—such are animals for St. Augustine. This attitude is somewhat understandable in that the Manichees were vegetarians, and St. Augustine, himself a Manichee for over a decade, wanted to divorce himself from this part of his past. He was right in suggesting that the vegetarianism of the Manichees was little else besides superstition. The elect, it was believed, could extract spiritual power from eating plants, and even here only under special conditions, but not from animals. But in the course of attacking the Manichees, St. Augustine was led to develop a general attitude toward human treatment of animals. After considering the swine that Jesus forced into the sea, St. Augustine suggests that even animal suffering means little or nothing to human beings.[5] Finally, animals are disassociated from us because of their lack of reason.[6]

The general animus against animals in the Judeo–Christian tradition is not without some exceptions, however. Ecclesiastes 3:19 suggests that human and beast share one breath, whatever that means in the context of the boiling kind. St. John Chrysostom held that saints should extend their gentleness even to unreasoning creatures.[7] Why only saints should be so gentle is unclear. Basil the Great composed a prayer for animals in which he indicated that God saves human beings *and* beasts.[8] And, of course, there is St. Francis of Assisi. His

Canticle to the Sun, where he preaches to the birds, is an attempt to exhort the birds to glorify God. But the following quotation from Peter Singer indicates that St. Francis' attitude towards animals, although an improvement over the traditional Judeo-Christian position regarding animals, nonetheless is problematic:

> While this kind of ecstatic universal love can be a wonderful fountain of compassion and goodness, the lack of rational reflection can also do much to counteract its beneficial consequences. If we love rocks, trees, plants, larks, and oxen equally, we may lose sight of the essential differences between them, most importantly, the differences in degree of sentience. We may then think that since we have to eat to survive, and since we cannot eat without killing something we love, it does not matter which we kill. Possibly it was for this reason that St. Francis' love for birds and oxen appears not to have led him to cease eating them; and when he drew up the rules for the conduct of the friars in the order he founded, he gave no instruction that they were to abstain from meat, except on certain feast days.[9]

Hartshorne will come to the aid of Franciscan sympathy for animals with some much-needed reflection and argument.

The intellectual framework that supports the dominant Christian view of animals is best exhibited in the writings of St. Thomas Aquinas. In *Summa Contra Gentiles*, St. Thomas tries to provide a metaphysical support for the theological belief in human dominion, namely, the control human beings have over their actions, a control that animals lack.[10] Humans are, in a way, causes of their own behavior or, better, self-movers, whereas animals act as mere instruments for the welfare of human beings, presumably because animals are not self–movers. Because only intellectual nature is free, animals are naturally slaves because they are not rational. Intellectual creatures hold the highest place in the universe because they approach nearest the divine likeness, except for the angels. Therefore, St. Thomas concludes, all others exist for the sake of human beings.

Although St. Thomas goes into more depth on the nature of animals than any other medieval thinker, not even he really argues his case. His biblical and theological background apparently made argument unnecessary. Six points need to be made regarding this text: (1) Given St. Thomas's contention that animals have no control over their actions, one wonders what he would say about the practice, which must have existed in the thirteenth century, of chastising a dog that had relieved itself where is was not supposed to. (2) One could ask what does cause an animal to "move," if not itself as the cause, in a way that does not similarly "move" human beings. St. Thomas gives little, if any, indication. To say "nature" or "instinct" is to beg the question, since humans are also natural beings with instincts. Indeed, they are animals themselves. (3) It is not at all clear that animals lack rationality completely, as we will see. (4) Even if human beings do approach nearest the divine likeness, it does not follow that all beings "beneath" human beings are there for humans' sake. (5) There is quite a gap between suggesting that a being lacks freedom and rationality, assuming for a moment that animals lack these, and arguing that therefore it is a slave or mere instrument. And, finally, (6) because St. Thomas, following Aristotle, was wrong in defending the natural slavery of some human beings, which many Christians never fully rejected until the nineteenth century, one might be led to question whether or not the natural inferiority of animals is as intuitively obvious as St. Thomas seems to think.

In this same passage St. Thomas finds himself in a bind of sorts. When he contends that it is not wrong for human beings to make use of animals, either by killing or in any other way, he seems to be in conflict with some scriptural passages that forbid us to be cruel to animals; for example, not to kill a bird with its young. St. Thomas's "solution" is ingenious, and has remained popular ever since, as in Kant: it is wrong to be cruel to animals not because of the pain inflicted on them, but bcause it may lead one to be cruel to human beings.[11] However, it is hard to see how forbidding us to boil a kid in its mother's milk is in fact meant to prevent us from boiling human beings in their mothers' (or anyone's) milk.

The Judeo-Christian tradition, even for a sophicticated thinker like St. Thomas, has largely been speciesist. "Speciesism" refers to the attitude which allows the interests of one's own species to override the sometimes greater interests of other species.[12] An example of people's speciesism would be their considering the human desire for a luxury item (such as a seal coat) more important than the seal's suffering because the desire is that of a human. Even if animals are not rational in any way, which St. Thomas never demonstrates, and even if human beings most closely approximate the divine likeness, there is no reason to infer that animals are our slaves to be treated in any way whatsoever except those that may lead to cruelty to human beings. The issue of slavery is not raised here histrionically. Just as racism and sexism were once accepted even in the most intelligent of Christian circles, by then unmasked for the injustices that they are, so might the same be done for speciesism.

St. Thomas unthinkingly assumes that it is necessary to eat meat.[13] Although, along with St. Augustine, he may legitimately condemn Manichean thought, what reason does he have to suspect the health of the Manichees?

Naivety may not be a fault, but lack of charity is, especially for a Christian. God loves animals because God loves all things that exist (Wisdom 11:25). Yet human beings, for St. Thomas, could not be charitable to animals even if they wanted to.[14] This is for three reasons: (1) Charity is a kind of friendship, and we wish good for our friends, but animals are not capable of experiencing good. (2) Friendship is based on fellowship (for example, living together), and no animal can have fellowship with a human being. And (3) charity is based on the fellowship of everlasting happiness, which animals cannot gain.

Once again, several comments are in order: (1) It is not clear why we cannot condescend to show charity to animals when even God can. It should be remembered that Jesus commended his Father for caring even for a sparrow's fall (Matthew 10:28); this point was not lost on Hamlet, who alludes to this piece of scripture,[15] as does Hartshorne. (2) St. Thomas does not show why having the ability to possess good is necessary for one to be shown charity. The whole point to Christian *agape*, as opposed to passionate *eros*, is that it is a love which does not demand love in return. (3) Some animals do show fellowship to human beings. For example, there are many, very many, pets that do. And (4) it is not readily apparent why charity can only be given to those capable of eternal life.

If my criticism of the dominant Christian attitude toward animals seems harsh, it is because familiarity with the dominant attitude toward animals breeds annoyance, if not contempt. I suggest that there is no theological reason why Christianity had to take the course it did regarding animals. When hearts and minds are not given over to sharing our goods with animals, or at least to acting as stewards of God's bounty, but rather to enslavement, it is hard to see how one has not violated the law of *agape*. Stephen R. L. Clark in *The Moral Status of Animals* and Andrew Linzey in *Animal Rights: A Christian Assessment of Man's Treatment of Animals* do a service for Christianity by pointing out that the orthodox ought to be castigated for inventing a war against the beasts in order to give themselves a sense of their own identity as human beings made in God's image.[16] If I understand *agape* correctly, one need not put other beings down in order to have oneself in dignified worth in God's eye. But it is St. Thomas's view, not St. Francis' nor Clark's, that has held sway even in the nineteenth and twentieth centuries.

Pope Pius IX in the mid-nineteenth century refused to allow a Society for the Prevention of Cruelty to Animals to be established in Rome, on the grounds that to do so would imply that human beings have duties to animals.[17] Joseph Rickaby's famous Thomistic textbook *Moral Philosophy* (1892) in effect gives an apologia for such behavior.[18] He argues against the "so-called rights of animals." His stance is directed against the English animal rights supporters of the late nineteenth century, who included Henry Salt. As far as I know, no one has given a scholarly treatment of the debate between Rickaby and G. Tyrrell, another Jesuit, on the one hand, and Frances Power Cobbe, on the other. This is unfortunate, because the positon of the two Jesuits exhibits many of the pitfalls of speciesism, and is precisely the view to which Hartshorne's thoughts on animals are opposed.

Brute beasts, Rickaby argues, do not have understanding, hence are not persons, hence cannot have any rights. They are not autocentric, but are things, and we have no duties whatsoever to them. We may have duties about them, as we have duties about stones, such as not to throw them through our neighbor's window. That is, we must not harm animals when they are our neighbor's property. Nor should we show rage toward animals, for this is "a miserable way of showing off human pre-eminence, to torture poor brutes in malevolent glee at their pain and helplessness." Rickaby's use of the terms "torture" and "malevolent" may lead one to suspect that he has some sympathy for the animals themselves, but this seems unlikely. Rather, torture and malevolence dispose the perpetrators to be cruel also to human beings. Likewise, to annoy a brute for sport is "unworthy of man," but only because it disposes one to inhumanity toward one's own species. Rickaby makes it clear, however, that the converse is not to be relied on: "there have been cruel men who have made pets of the brute creation." In the pursuit of science, not only can we cause pain to animals, but we are not even bound "to any anxious care to make this pain as little as may be. Brutes are as *things* in our regard." They exist for us, not for themselves. Finally, for Rickaby, we cannot even preach kindness or charity to brutes as a primary obligation, for several reasons: man alone speaks, man alone hopes for and believes in God, etc. To be kind to animals is only an expression of our kindness to other human beings.

Tyrrell tries to clarify Rickaby's position and defend it against its attackers. By way of clarification, Tyrrell holds that although animals may have a sort of sensibility (*verstand*), they do not have the entire power of perceiving and conceiving (*vernunft*), which is a "sign and normal output" of human personality (711). *Vernunft*, or "pure reason," does not constitute personality, but because it is only the spiritual soul which is capable of manifesting *vernunft*, animals are in a sense equal to "stocks and stones" (711, 715). Tyrrell also tries to clarify Rickaby's position by saying that vivisection can only be supported in the abstract, but in that the practical conditions of the laboratory are "easily liable to abuse" (709)—he is, in a way, an anti-vivisectionist; again, not because of any "quasi-personality or quasi-rights in brute beasts." The key to Tyrrell's position lies in the following quotation:

> Pain, therefore, like pleasure, is to be estimated in importance, not merely by its intensity and quality, but by the dignity and circumstances of the subject suffering. . . . The pain of a man, even though identical in kind and intensity with that of a brute, is a greater pain, insomuch as it is the pain of an indefinitely higher creature, (709).

That is, rights are common to every person as person (over and above which the person may have many other rights as well). As with Rickaby, we have no duties to animals, although we do have duties concerning them. One of these duties for Tyrrell (contra Rickaby) is "that of not inflicting pain on them directly, nor even indirectly, without proportionate justifying cause" (711). We will later see this statement come back to haunt Tyrrell.

Tyrrell goes on to say that if the essential difference between man and brute is denied, then either anthropophagy (eating human beings) will be allowed or we may not kill and eat nonhuman animals under any circumstances. Tyrrell calls this the *reductio ad absurdum* of Cobbe's position. In that the latter alternative seems unthinkable to Tyrrell, he believes that Cobbe has given up on the inviolable dignity of human life, such that murder, infanticide, and the like can no longer be prohibited (712). He says, in reference to Cobbe, with tongue in cheek, that "zoophilists are not always charitable" (713). To sum up, only a person is the subject of rights and duties, and animals are not persons. They are lent to us by God for our use, and we have duties towards God concerning them. God intends for them "a certain 'sweetness' of non-intellectual life" (714–715).

There are so many questions that can be raised concerning the Rickaby-Tyrrell stance that I hardly know where to begin. Let me offer two arguments for animal rights that have been used in the contemporary debate in philosophical circles concerning animals so as to show the inadequacy of the Rickaby-Tyrrell stance. Later I will move on to Cobbe.

In abbreviated form, the argument from sentiency goes something like this:

(1) Any being that can suffer has at the very least the right not to be forced to suffer unnecessarily.

(2) It is not necessary that we inflict suffering on animals so that we can eat, because eating vegetables can be perfectly healthy.

(3) Therefore, to inflict unnecessary suffering on an animal in order to eat it is morally reprehensible or cruel.

The question is not, "Can they reason? nor "Can they talk?", but "Can they suffer?" Animals raised for the table can; plants, for all we can tell, cannot (I will argue for these claims later). Some might suspect that an escape from this argument can be found in "sneaking up" on the animal to kill it painlessly. There are many ways to respond to this objection, one of which is the argument from marginal cases. (It does seem peculiar that some think pain is a "hurt" but killing is not.) Peter Singer puts it this way:

> The catch is that any such characteristic that is possessed by *all* human beings will not be possessed *only* by human beings. For example all humans, but not only humans, are capable of feeling pain; and while only humans are capable of solving complex mathematical problems, not all humans can do this. So it turns out that in the only sense in which we can truly say, as an assertion of fact, that all humans are equal, at least some members of other species are also "equal"—equal, that is, to some humans.[19]

Theological statements of a human being's privileged status cannot be philosophically justified. But to say that we can legitimately eat animals because human beings are rational, or autonomous, or religious believers, or language users, etc., does not in fact refer to all human beings. These "marginal cases" include infants, the mentally feeble, and the like. If we "lower" our standard to that of sentiency (for example, the ability to experience pain) so as to protect these people, we must also protect many animals, including those that we eat.

Or as Tom Regan puts it, if an animal has characteristics $a, b, c \ldots n$, but lacks autonomy (or reason, and so on), and if a human being has characteristics $a, b, c \ldots n$, but lacks autonomy (or reason, etc.) then we have just as much reason to believe that the animal has rights as the human. These rights would include the right not to be forced to suffer or be killed unnecessarily.

I will now list, with these arguments as a background, thirteen problems with the Rickaby-Tyrrell stance.

(1) Rickaby offers no evidence to show that animals lack understanding. Tyrrell's distinction between *verstand* and *vernunft* helps somewhat, but both men fail to do justice to animal intelligence, which even in their day had received a significant amount of study.

(2) Even if animals lack understanding (whatever that means), it is not at all clear why they cannot have rights. Rickaby-Tyrrell state, again without

argument, that only persons can have rights, even though many persons do not have understanding, or religious beliefs, or language. The argument from marginal cases is instructive here.

(3) Rickaby-Tyrrell might avoid these arguments by seeking refuge in certain theological doctrines, for example, humanity's being created in God's image, or the human being's possession of an immortal soul. I say "might," because Rickaby implies that understanding is a necessary condition for personhood, hence the possession of rights. For him, animals have no rights because they have no understanding. And Tyrrell holds that *vernunft* is the "normal output" of human beings. If he includes (abnormal?) human beings without *vernunft* in the category of rights-holders, then perhaps he should also be willing to include some animals. In any event, to exalt human beings' theological status, it is not necessary to denigrate that of animals to mere thinghood. And to say that the mentally enfeebled human being has rights, whereas the animal does not, because the mentally enfeebled *is* a human being begs the question as to why only human beings can have rights.

(4) Rickaby's bifurcation of species into persons and things seems too rigid. To lump animals with stones, as Rickaby-Tyrrell do, fails to do justice to the significant differences among, say, a stone, a tree, an oyster, and a cow. Their knowledge of Aristotelian psychology, at the very least, should have prevented them from making such a rigid bifurcation.

(5) Rickaby shows a poor word choice when he says we should not "torture" animals because of duties we have to other human beings. Surely any being that has the capacity to be tortured (for example, cows, not stones nor asparagus) ought not to be tortured whether or not other human beings will be attacked later by the torturer.

(6) If Rickaby does mean to use the word "torture," it is unclear how he can say that we are not bound to make the pain animals experience for the sake of science as minimal as possible. One meaning of "torture" is the infliction of unnecessary pain.

(7) Even if human beings alone speak, hope, believe in God, as Rickaby states, not all human beings can do these things. Again, the argument from marginal cases raises its head.

(8) Tyrrell's point regarding the necessity of considering the dignity of the subject that is suffering is well put, but largely irrelevant. To hold, as Tyrrell does, that a pain equal in intensity and quality is a more important and a greater pain when it is a human being's experience as opposed to an animal does not show that animal suffering is not important or great, nor that animals cannot be the loci of rights. All that Tyrrell has shown is that animal suffering is not

as important as human suffering, and that animal rights are not as important as human rights. He has not shown that animals cannot have rights.

(9) Tyrrell refutes his own case when he contends that we have a duty concerning animals (but not to them) to not inflict pain on them without proportionate justifying cause. Yet Tyrrell is "ashamed to elaborate such obvious platitudes" (711). The fact that we need proportionate justifying cause when we slit the throat of a sheep but not when we hit a stone indicates that sheep are not mere things. Tyrrell's admission of the need for proportionate justifying cause perhaps should have made Tyrrell a vegetarian even if we have no duties *to* animals. Contrary to certain myths regarding idyllic conditions "down on the farm" and in the abattoir (slaughterhouse), animals raised for the table do suffer when raised and killed for profit; it is only a short step from being a mere thing to serving as a commodity. Why do we kill animals? Not because we have to, as the healthiness of millions of vegetarians proves. Because they taste good? Is "aesthetic necessity" a proportionate justifying cause for inflicting suffering on and killing an animal? Hardly.

(10) To say that animals have the right not to be forced to suffer or be killed unnecessarily does not, as Tyrrell implies, deny the difference between human and nonhuman animals. And even if such a denial of a moral difference were made, it would not necessarily follow that it would be legitimate to kill and eat human beings. Tyrrell's position is especially weak here.

(11) If animals do have rights we are not giving up on the inviolable dignity of human life, as Tyrrell states. Tyrrell erroneously seems to think that rights constitute a pie of a fixed size, so that by giving a slice to animals there is less for human beings. To say that the animal rightist cannot be opposed to anthropophagy or infanticide is demagoguery on Tyrrell's part.

(12) Tyrrell is correct, however, that zoophilists like Cobbe are not always charitable. But neither are meat-eaters, Catholics, atheists, or Albanians.

(13) Finally, one wonders how Tyrrell knows that God intends animals for the "sweetness" of a life at the disposal of human beings. Could this "sweetness" be a rationalization for Tyrrell's own culturally influenced culinary habits?

Cobbe, on the other hand, shows an awareness of the aforementioned arguments for animal rights, and avoids the syrupy sentimentalism that plagues much literature on the topic. But the zoophile (animal-lover) faces the peril that Singer noticed in his treatment of St. Francis. Cobbe clearly avoids this danger. She does not plead for equal rights for animals with human beings. Rather:

> We Zoophilists . . . are pretty well agreed that the chasm between the human race and non-human animals—though vast in itself and sufficient to create essential differences between moral relations of Man and Man and those between Man and Brute—is yet *not* sufficient to cut short the moral obligations of man at the confines of humanity. (503)

So also, the argument from sentiency forces Cobbe to realize that there are gradations in the animal world itself, such that her case weakens as she goes "down" the evolutionary scale from mammals or birds to fish, and then to other edible sea creatures. As Singer has it:

> Those who want to be absolutely certan that they are not causing suffering will not eat mollusks either; but somewhere between a shrimp and an oyster seems as good a place to draw the line as any, and better than most.[20]

Cobbe herself talks about:

> such vast differences between the species of animals in their descending ranks— vertebrates and invertebrates, mammals, birds, reptiles, fishes, molluscs, insects, down to zoophytes and bacilli—that an analogous difference must exist in our moral relations to each class. (503)

Rickaby and Tyrrell, however, as Cobbe notices, refuse:

> to draw any line whatever between those highest brutes and the inferior grades of animal life, between an elephant and an oyster, between an anthropoid ape and a flea. (503)

They are all just things. Cobbe even shows an awareness of the argument from marginal cases when, in a criticism of Rickaby's position regarding understanding, she states that:

> I do not know that we find much *intellectus* or pure reason in a baby of a year old, or in a cannibal savage. (500)

Yet she recognizes that the baby and the savage have rights.

Another difference between Cobbe, on the one hand, and Rickaby-Tyrrell, on the other, is her belief that animals can be shown Christian love. Rickaby, citing St. Thomas favorably, denies that we can show love *(caritas)*, a type of friendship, to animals. As before, three reasons are given by St. Thomas. First, friendship means that we will good for our friend, and animals cannot receive goodness because they are not rational. Second, all friendship is founded on some community of life, but irrational creatures can have no share in human life. And third, love is based on a sharing in eternal happiness.

What St. Thomas (and Rickaby) leave unexplained are: (1) how we can, on their criteria, still show love to human beings who are not rational; (2) how we can still show friendship to human beings with whom we do not live in community; (3) why community of sentient life could not be a criterion of association needed for love as opposed to a community of rational agents; (4) why a sharing in eternal happiness is needed for love; and (5) how Thomistic *caritas* is compatible with Christian *agape*, which does not demand love in return.

Cobbe agrees with Tyrrell that too much attention is paid "these days" to bodily as compared to spiritual interests, which is why those for animal rights denounce the materialism that attaches so disproportionate an importance to the supposed welfare of our own species. It is the spiritual or moral part of human beings which is sacred, Cobbe argues (504). Because we have a prior claim upon us by other human beings does not mean that we have no time left for animals, especially when charity can be extended to them through *abstinence from* certain practices (506). Again, Tyrrell misses the point when he warns Cobbe not to "leave the ministry of one's husband and children in order to serve poodles, or to found hospitals for hungry cats while Christians are starving in our streets." [21] What both Tyrrell and Cobbe could not realize is that one of the major reasons why there are people starving in the world (millions of them now, most of them non-Christian) is the inefficient use of grain in the meat industry.[22]

In this analysis of a particular historical debate I may have given the impression of biting off more than I can chew; but I have not intended in this chapter anything like an adequate foundation for Christian or Catholic moral theory regarding animals. I prefer to think of this chapter as a prolegomenon to Hartshorne's more systematic treatment of these same problems.

The reason why this nineteenth-century debate is a good place to start is that many have the impression that this is where Christian thought on animals ends. Charles Magel identifies Rickaby's stance with the "view of Catholicism."[23] Peter Singer notes that the Thomistic position of Rickaby (and the similar views of Austin Fagothy and Vernon Bourke) has remained the "official position" of the Catholic Church to this day.[24] The fact that the Thomistic stance on animals is still dominant can be exemplified in many ways. One source is Pope John Paul II's otherwise commendable encyclical, "On Human Work."[25] Repeatedly he emphasizes the human duty to "subdue, to dominate the earth." This duty has a wide range, as John Paul II admits, because it allows human beings to use all the resources of th earth (including animals) for human ends. This point of view is what allows anti-Catholics like Cobbe (as opposed to non-Catholics) to say about Rickaby that:

> My main contention against the Jesuit moralist is this: That discussions about rights, as between us and animals, are purely scholastic pedantry when we have the higher law of love to inspire us with divine sympathy and pity for all suffering. (499)

The same could be said of most Protestant theologians' views on animals, as Linzey notices. If followers of Jesus are not concerned with all suffering, what are they concerned about?

The sadness in all this is that Christianity does have the resources to deal fairly with animals, as Hartshorne shows. Even Rickaby reluctantly admits that morality may advance beyond St. Thomas.[26] More positive is the approach taken by Henry David Thoreau, the American nineteenth- century vegetarian who influenced English zoophiles like Cobbe and Henry Salt:

> I have no doubt that it is part of the destiny of the human race, in its gradual improvement, to leave off eating animals, as surely as the savage tribes have left off eating each other when they came into contact with the more civilized.[27]

There are continents and seas in the moral world yet unexplored, and each person is an isthmus to that world, but:

> How worn and dusty, then, must be the highways of the world, how deep the ruts of tradition and conformity![28]

If Hartshorne had to cut a completely new path so as to bisect the worn highway of animal denigration, his task would be close to impossible. But because the Christian God is a God of love, and presumably always has been, Hartshorne's path is at least partially cleared already, such that his job is more that of a co-laborer on a project whose completion demands a vast cosmic epoch.[29]

Admittedly, this is only a thumbnail sketch of the history of Jewish and Christian thought on animals, but such sketches can be accurate and useful. It is by no means clear that a more detailed history would yield more substantive results. Let me cite a few Jewish and Christian authors to make this point.

Earlier in this century Louis Ginsberg and Paul Shorey rightfully criticized an article in *The Nation* which blindly followed Schopenhauer's claim that Judaism had no regard for the feelings of animals.[30] They were astute to quote Proverbs (12:10) to the effect that a righteous person does regard the life of his animals (note the possessive). But how should the righteous person show such regard? Granted, there are an abundance of legal provisions in Scripture that would have made a Society for the Prevention of Cruelty to Animals superfluous in biblical times, and would even have prohibited hunting or any other "wrongful" human treatment of a creature merely because it was a member of a different species. The problem is that what it means to these thinkers "to wrong" a creature is remarkably truncated.

Louis Berman, in his book *Vegetarianism and the Jewish Tradition,* may be correct that there is a tendency in Judaism toward vegetarianism and a serious concern for individual animals; he is certainly correct that the Jewish tradition has often not lived up to its ideals regarding animals.[31] His position is far more acceptable for animal rightists than that of J. David Bleich, who admittedly does a fine job of isolating those biblical passages and pieces of rabbinical scholarship (especially those of Maimonides) that encourage measures be taken to alleviate *tza'ar ba'alei hayyim*: the pain of living creatures. But Bleich does not seem to be bothered by the fact that the laws regarding "animal welfare" are not necessarily designed primarily to promote the welfare of animals; rather, these laws are often rooted in a concern for the financial loss that would occur if animals were abused. As in St. Thomas, we only have duties concerning animals, not to them. Hence, the slaughter of animals is permitted, as is the infliction of pain if the act is designed to further a "legitimate" human purpose. What is "legitimate" is not explicated by Bleich.

One wonders if it is enough, as Bleich thinks, for a religion to merely allow adherents to show respect to animals.[32] As I will argue, a religion should at least encourage such respect, if not require it. The inadequacy of merely allowing what Bleich calls "stringencies of piety" can be seen when *shehitah* (ritualized Jewish slaughter) is considered. Bleich is convinced that this method is "the most humane method of slaughter known to man," yet even he has to admit that when the carotid arteries and jugular veins are severed "the resultant loss of blood causes the animal to become unconscious *in a matter of seconds*" (emphasis supplied). The scientific study Bleich himself cites in favor of his claim that the animal may not experience pain in the *shehitah* actually leaves open the possibility of quite intense pain for between 3.3 to 6.2 seconds.[33]

Andrew Linzey, an Anglican, and James Gaffney, a Catholic, try to do in an analogous way for Christianity what Berman tries to do for Judaism. That is, they admit the dominant anthropocentrism of their religious tradition, but suggest that such a stance was not necessary within the tradition and actually falls short of the tradition's best thoughts on animals. Both (along with Jurgen Moltmann) would agree with Berman that the notion of a sabbath rest should include serious reflection on how to avoid the seemingly endless exploitation of animals and the rest of nature.

Linzey emphasizes the idea that, because on orthodox Christian grounds creatures were made by God, they must be somewhat holy and not mere instruments for our use, as many Christians have assumed.[34] Ascribing absolute value to human beings or ascribing hardly any value to animals are flip sides of the same heresy. Human dominion, for Linzey, means stewardship. Even if meat eating is sanctioned in Genesis (9:3), it is only permitted as a concession to human sinfulness; and even if human beings could legitimately use animals, it should nonetheless be realized that such use is not the animal's only reason for existing. The problem with Linzey's position, from a metaphysical point of view, is that it is not clear how his conception of God can accomodate his principles in Christian ethics dealing with animals. For example, how can Linzey say both that "God does not need creation" *and* that "creation . . . must be valuable to him"? And how can he say both that, "Because it is ontologically distinct from him [God], creation occupies a separate sphere of existence," *and* that, "This objective reality must be such that God can participate within it, . . . the divine presence can incarnate itself within it"?[35] It is precisely these sorts of problems that I will treat later, especially in Chapter Two.

Gaffney's discussions are:

> not intended to suggest that Roman Catholic tradition evidences any strong, unbroken strand of interest in the moral status of nonhuman animals. They are rather to suggest that Catholics might have found, as a few still do find among their acknowledged classics, some stimulation for the rational and even pious cultivation of such interest.[36]

Note the word "might" in the above quotation. Because the modern renewal of interest in animals as recipients of human morality arose chiefly as the result of nineteenth-century liberalism, which was chiefly associated with secularism, the Catholic response to such interest was "typically defensive," with only grudging approval eventually given for animal protection.

In very recent years, however, there have been a few changes in Christianity which will perhaps allow Catholic thought to drift toward the Franciscan pole of its tradition regarding animals rather than toward the Thomistic pole. One such factor is the appeal to human dignity—rather than to rationality—as the foundation of moral regard. Although this appeal can be used in an anthropocentric way, the fact that a being can be seen as dignified without evincing rationality makes possible the inclusion of animals into the region of moral concern via the arguments from sentiency and marginal cases.

The Islamic approach to animals is very much like the Jewish and Christian approaches, As in Judaism, there are scriptural prohibitions against mistreating animals in the Koran and instructional corollaries to scripture offered by holy men (*hadith*). Muslim jurists (*muftis*) have further amplified these two sources.[37] Although in Islam the real criterion for human superiority over animals is not rationality—consisting instead in *taquwah* or spiritual volition— there is still a conception of human superiority which allows the slaughter of animals. Even if killing animals for sport or luxury is prohibited (as in Judaism), animals may be killed for food, as if meat itself were not a luxury in regions where vegetable food is abundant, as it is in many Muslim areas. One's regret with regard to Islam is analogous to that for Judaism and Christianity, in that Muslims too could have (I daresay should have) worked their way to the vegetarian position. Consider the following declaration made by Muhammed himself, analogous to Jesus' famous remark treated by Hartshorne.

> There is no man who kills [even] a sparrow or anything beyond that, *without it deserving it*, but God will ask him about it (emphasis added).[38]

Obviously the situation changes somewhat when Eastern religions are considered, but their thought regarding animals is often more complex than many would suspect. In Hinduism, for example, the recommendation to cultivate a kind attitude toward animals is not based on considerations about the animal as such, but on how the development of this attitude is a part of the purification process leading to *moksa* (salvation).[39] Even the virtue of *ahimsa* (nonviolence) refers to something that merely has value to the extent that it enables the seeker to climb the rungs of the ladder to *moksa*. Hence one can easily understand the traditional Hindu practice of animal sacrifice: the animal sacrificed in ritual is not really an animal but a symbol; only the outward appearance comes to an end, not the *atman* (inner self). And one can also understand why *ahimsa,* although present in every phase of Hinduism's development, is less prominent than it is in Jainism and Buddhism.

It must be granted that Hinduism encourages us to see human affinity to nature, including animals, as do most Eastern religions. This affinity has obvious consequences for the Hindu beliefs on pets as family members and the sacredness of cows. Yet because *ahimsa* is not a *dharma* (duty) to other animals, but a way to develop self-restraint, there are only duties about animals rather than duties to them. This is very close to the theoretical stance concerning animals found in St. Thomas, although it is important to note that human beings practically speaking would have more duties with respect to animals in Hinduism than in Christianity because Hinduism considers it possible for a human being to be reborn as an animal, or an animal to be reborn as a human being. Yet because *himsa* (violence) can be recommended in our treatment of animals if its "benefits" outweigh its liabilities, the practical superiority of Hinduism to traditional Christianity regarding animals is slighter than some would think.

The most distinctive and commendable features of Hindu thought on animals are those that it has borrowed from Jainism and Buddhism. Although both of these religions have been associated with belief in transmigration, neither has based respect for animals exclusively on that belief. In this respect they are like many of the ancient Greek vegetarians. That is, both Jainism and Buddhism acknowledge duties *to* animals. This is what makes them different from Hinduism, as does the fact that these religions have always avoided animal sacrifice.

It is important for the purposes of this book to emphasize that Hartshorne's thought on God and animals not only tries to improve upon the insights of Judaism and Christianity, but also borrows from the Buddhist (and, I allege, Jain) tradition.

> At the heart of Jainism is the doctrine that all being *(sat)* is divided into nonliving *(ajiva)* and living *(jiva)* forms. The former includes what we might consider principles: motion, rest, space, matter, and time. The latter, the living forms, includes almost everything regarded as animate or inanimate by non-Jainas.[40]

This is very close to Hartshorne's view that only the most abstract entities do not become, and that every other concrete entity displays some activity. This belief in nature as alive obviously needs subtle treatment, so as to avoid some common caricatures of panpsychism. But such a belief, which is favorable indeed toward animals, is ably defended by Hartshorne, as we will see.

It is no accident that vegetarianism is required of all Jains. Although small in number, they have had a great deal of influence on other Indian religions, including Buddhism, which provides the route through which most Westerners come into contact with Jain ideas. Although Jainism and Buddhism largely agree about animals, the latter does not posit an abiding life force *(jiva)*, but asserts that all phenomena are without a lasting self-nature. The bondage of action *(karma)* causes the cyclic wheel of existence *(samsara)* to continually turn. Thus, the goal for the Hartshornian thinker, under the influence of Buddhism, should be to do away with the strict unity of an animal's experience through time—in that "personal" identity is a matter of degree for animals and even human beings—*and* at the same time preserve some feeling for the individual animal *as* individual, so as not to defend cruelty. It is always *this* particular pig which suffers, not pighood. Because of Hartshorne's asymmetrical theory of time, to be treated later, he is able to do justice to both of these poles.

Although vegetarianism is not a strict requirement for all Buddhists, nor even for all monastic Buddhist communities, it is nonetheless a common practice and some version of the precept not to needlessly harm living things *(pranatipatad viratih)* is central to all Buddhist sects. And as before, this precept as it affects the use of animals for food or in laboratories can be defended on grounds quite apart from belief in reincarnation.

> A modern reading of *karma*, which would dispose of the need for belief in reincarnation and hence be more accessible to the superstition-wary Westerner, would be to view it as horizontal instead of sequential. An action does not necessarily remain confined to one life, but its influence spreads out to the lives of others. If one acts violently and is imprisoned as a result, an entire family is affected. Similarly . . . the rise of science gave birth to medicines and luxuries that have greatly eased human misery. But these same advances now plague the world with nuclear weaponry and chemical warfare, increased rates of cancer and heart disease, and tragedies such as thalidomide and Agent Orange. It might be said that the violence that was required for the development of these various substances is now being experienced indirectly as the widespread effects of the technological age are being felt.[41]

The avoidance of death is not the purpose or *telos* for Buddhism, but it should be noted that the quality of life and the quality of death *are* most important for Buddhist thinkers.[42] Hence, the Buddhist belief in the nonsubstantiality and impermanence of animal life does not prevent its opposition to the various cruel ways of treating and killing animals.

An important similarity between what seems to have been the Buddha's own thinking and Hartshorne's is that human beings can have fellow-feeling for other loci of feeling in the world, which we can know are distinct from our own. To put it in Hartshorne's terms, this similarity is based on an epistemological realism and a metaphysical idealism. A famous example of this similarity from the Buddha's own life was his coming to the aid of a swan wounded by a hunter. We can know that the swan is different from us and that the swan can certainly feel.[43]

The solace received by the animal rightist when considering Jainism and Buddhism, and to a lesser extent in Hinduism, however, does not extend to Confucianism. Rodney Taylor does a fine job of defending Confucianism against the traditional charge that it is just another type of anthropocentrism, but it is hard to see how this traditional accusation can be totally dismissed. The *Analects* of Confucius make it clear that the primary task for a human being is to restore or maintain the moral order that once prevailed in China; this task supervenes on the lives of animals, which are "totally secondary."[44] Ritual and decorum rule over sensitivity to animals, the latter of which is supererogatory, above and beyond the call of duty. Mo Tzu, a thinker of the fifth century B.C., makes a legitimate point (implied in Aristotle) when he notices that if we are exhorted to show universal love, there will be no love at all because it would have no beginning. But we need not infer that this insight works against the zoophile's case if such a case is based on the respect due to individual, particular animals; for example, this sheep here about to be killed or that one there on the dinner table.

Although Neoconfucianism from the tenth century A.D. on continues to teach in the traditional anthropocentric vein of Confucianism, there is an increased emphasis on the unity of nature. To the extent that one emphasizes the Great Ultimate *(T'ai-chi)*, composed of the intermingling forces of *yin* and *yang*, one establishes a vision of unity that could bridge the supposedly vast gulf between human beings and animals. (Hartshorne bridges this gulf with his Platonic notion of God as the World Soul, which is similar to the Eastern notion of a unified nature.) Even the ancient Confucian interpreter Mencius, however, had noticed "That whereby man differs from the lower animals is but small . . . The mass of people [unwittingly] cast it away, while superior men preserve it."[45] A brilliant insight, I think, and a favorite of Thoreau's.[46] It is also an insight implicit in Hartshorne's own thought. Thus, Confucianism (along with Judaism, Christianity, Islam, and Hinduism) has an unrealized potential within its perspective to develop a humane conception of animals.

One of the glories of Hartshorne's thought is that it attempts to incorporate (within the Christian tradition, of course) the best insights of Western theism and Eastern pantheism, which not only helps us better understand the place of animals in creation, but also enables us to better understand God on the analogy of a cosmic animal or a World Soul for the body of the world when conceived as a unified whole. In order to exhibit the glory of this synthesis, I will first in Chapter Two have to treat Hartshorne's "dipolar" logic, a logic that he uses to isolate which attributes are divine.

Chapter Two

God and Noninvidious Contrasts

> *And God and Man divided, as they ought*
> *Between them the great system of the world*
> *Where man is sphered, and which God animates . . .*
> *But 'tis God*
> *Diffused through all, that doth make all one whole . . .*
> *Such outrage done to nature as compels*
> *The indignant power to justify herself,*
> *Yea, to avenge her violated rights.*

The purpose of this chapter is not to explicate Hartshorne's defense of belief in the existence of God, a defense which is largely based on the ontological argument. Rather, assuming that God exists, we shall ask two questions: What is the *mode* of God's existence? And how does the divine mode of existence affect our understanding of animals?

We shall see that Hartshorne's theory differs from that of classical theism, the philosophical position that lies behind traditional defense of Christianity (for example, St. Augustine, St. Thomas, the Protestant Reformers, Kant) (see PS), Judaism (Philo, Maimonides), and Islam (Avicenna, Averroes). Nonetheless, Hartshorne calls his position "neoclassical theism" in that he shows some debt to classical theism, especially St. Anselm's version. Neoclassical theism is different from Eastern pantheism, but not to the extent that Hartshorne cannot incorporate an Eastern concern for animals. He calls his synthesis "panentheism", as we shall see.

Hartshorne fully accepts the position of the traditional Christian philosophers, that is, that logical analysis is in the service of a higher end. In his concern for the *meaning* of "God" he is what P. F. Strawson would call a "revisionary metaphysician," one who is very much concerned with the language we use to describe God. But Hartshorne holds that the classical theist's conception of God is internally incoherent. Throughout his career much of

Hartshorne's work has attempted to show this incoherence. One of the major criticisms Hartshorne has against classical theism in philosophy and theology (as opposed to biblical theism) is that it either explicitly or implicitly identifies God as active and not passive. St. Thomas's unmoved mover is the most obvious example of this tendency, but in general all classical theists see God as a timeless, supernatural being that does not change. The classical theist's inconsistency lies in also claiming that God knows and loves. For example, if God knows, God must be a subject on the analogy of human subjects, even if divine knowing is connected with divine willing; and if God is a subject who knows, then God must be affected by, be passive with respect to, the object known.

According to Colin Gunton, Hartshorne commits the opposite error of making God into something very close to a purely passive deity.[1] Although Gunton seems to agree with Hartshorne's attack on classical theism for its lack of concern for divine passivity, he disagrees with what he believes is Hartshorne's own lack of concern for divine activity. One of the purposes of this chapter is to defend Hartshorne against Gunton, so as to show in a preliminary way how Hartshorne's dipolar theism, to be explained later, affects how we can talk about animals in relation to God.[2] In Chapter Three, having treated the ways various religions have thought about animals (Chapter One) and Hartshorne's theory of God (Chapter Two), I shall be in a position to analyze how Hartshorne's theory of God can improve on these religions' previous understanding of animals.

It will be to our advantage to get as clear as we can on what we mean by the term "God." For Hartshorne, the term refers to the supremely excellent or all-worshipful being (PS; 1). As is well known, Hartshorne has been the most important defender in this century of St. Anselm's ontological argument for the existence of God, and his debt to St. Anselm is evident in this preliminary definition. It closely resembles St. Anselm's "that than which no greater can be conceived." Yet the ontological argument is not what is at stake here.

Even if the argument fails, which Hartshorne would doubt, the preliminary definition of God as the supremely excellent being, the all-worshipful being, or the greatest conceivable being seems unobjectionable. To say that God can be defined in these ways still leaves open the possibility that God is even more excellent or worshipful than our ability to conceive. This allows us to avoid objections from classical theists or mystics who fear that by defining God we are limiting God to "merely" human language. Hartshorne is simply suggesting that when we think of God we must be thinking of a being who surpasses all others, or else we are not thinking of God. Even the atheist or agnostic would admit this much. When the atheist says, "There is no God," he is denying that a supremely excellent, all-worshipful, greatest conceivable being exists.

The contrast excellent–inferior is the truly invidious contrast when applied to God (PS; 4). If to be invidious is to be injurious, then this contrast is the most invidious one of all when both terms are applied to God, because God is only excellent. God is inferior in no way. Period. To suggest that God is in some small way inferior to some other being is no longer to speak about God but about some being that is not supremely excellent, all-worshipful, or the greatest conceivable. Hartshorne's major criticism of classical theism is that it has assumed that all contrasts, or most of them, when applied to God are invidious.

Let us assume that God exists. What attributes does God possess? Consider the following two columns of attributes in polar contrast to each other.

one	many
being	becoming
activity	passivity
permanence	change
necessity	contingency
self-sufficient	dependent
actual	potential
absolute	relative
abstract	concrete

Classical theism tends toward oversimplification. It is comparatively easy to say, "God is strong rather than weak, so in all relations God is active, not passive." In each case, the classical theist decides which member of the contrasting pair is good (on the left), then attributes it to God, while wholly denying the contrasting term (on the right). Hence, God is one, but not many; permanent but not changing, etc. This leads to what Hartshorne calls the monopolar prejudice. Monopolarity is common to both classical theism and pantheism, with the major difference between the two being the fact that classical theism admits the reality of plurality, potentiality, and becoming as a secondary form of existence "outside" God (on the right), whereas in pantheism God includes all reality within itself. Common to both classical theism and pantheism is the belief that the categorical contrasts listed above are invidious. The dilemma these two positions face is that either the deity is only one constituent of the whole (classical theism) or else the alleged inferior pole in each contrast (on the right) is illusory (pantheism).

For Hartshorne this dilemma is artificial. It is produced by the assumption that exellence is found by separating and purifying one pole (on the left) and denigrating the other (on the right). That this is not the case can be seen by analyzing some of the attributes in the right-hand column. At least since St. Augustine, classical theists have been convinced that God's eternity meant not that God endured through all time, but that God was outside of time altogether, and was not, could not be receptive to temporal change. St. Thomas, following Aristotle, who was the greatest predecessor to classical theism, identified God as unmoved. Yet both activity and passivity can be either good or bad. Good passivity is likely to be called sensitivity, responsiveness, adaptability, sympathy, and the like. Insufficiently subtle or defective passivity is called wooden inflexibility, mulish stubbornness, inadaptability, unresponsiveness, and the like. "Passivity" per se refers to the way in which an individual's activity takes account of, and renders itself appropriate to, the activities of others (PS; 2). (This instructive definition of divine passivity should be kept in mind when we consider Gunton's criticisms of Hartshorne.) To deny God passivity altogether is to deny God those aspects of passivity that are excellences. Or again, to altogether deny God the ability to change does avoid fickleness, but at the expense of the ability to lovingly react to the suffering of others, whether human *or* animal others.

The terms on the left side also have both good and bad aspects as well. Oneness can mean wholeness; but also it can mean monotony or triviality. Actuality can mean definiteness; or it can mean nonrelatedness to others.

What happens to divine love when God, according to St. Thomas, is claimed to be *pure* actuality? God ends up loving the world, but is not intrinsically related to it, whatever sort of love that may be. Self–sufficiency can, at times, be selfishness.

The trick when thinking of God, for Hartshorne, is to attribute to God all excellences (left and right sides together)—hence Hartshorne calls his position "dual transcendence"—and not to attribute to God any inferiorities (of the right or left sides). In short, excellent–inferior, knowledge–ignorance, or good–evil are invidious contrasts, but one–many, being–becoming, et al., are noninvidious contrasts. Gunton is helpful on why evil is not a category and need not be applied to God. It is not a category because it is not universal; it is not universal because animals cannot commit it, even if they can be its victims. That is, both animals and God can feel evil but they cannot commit it, God because of the supreme goodness in the divine nature, animals because of their ignorance of moral principles. (PS; 15) (This is not the last time their paths will cross in the distinction between aesthetic and moral evil.)

Unlike classical theism and pantheism, Hartshorne's theism is dipolar. To be specific, within each pole of a nonvidious contrast (for example, permanence–change), there are invidious or injurious elements (inferior permanence or inferior change), but also noninvidious, good elements (excellent permanence or excellent change).

Hartshorne does not believe in two gods, one unified and the other plural, and so forth. Rather, he believes that what are often thought to be contraries are really mutually interdependent correlatives:

> The good as we know it is unity-in-variety, or variety-in-unity; if the variety overbalances, we have chaos or discord; if the unity, we have monotony or triviality. (PS; 3)

Supreme excellence, to be truly so, must somehow be able to integrate all the complexity there is in the world into itself as one spiritual whole. The word "must" indicates divine necessity, along with God's essence, which is to necessarily exist. And the word "complexity" indicates the contingency that affects God through creaturely decisions. But in the classical theistic view, God is solely identified with the stony immobility of the absolute, implying nonrelatedness to the world. For Hartshorne, God in its abstract nature, God's being, may in a way escape from the temporal flux, but a living God is related to the world of becoming, which entails a divine becoming as well, if the world is in some way internally related to God. The classical theist's alternative to this view suggests that all relationships to God are external to divinity, once again threatening not only God's love, but also God's nobility. A dog's being behind a particular rock affects the dog in certain ways; thus this relation is an internal relation to the dog. But it does not affect the rock, whose relationship with the dog is external to the rock's nature. (PS; 4; IO; 55) Does this not show the superiority of canine consciousness, which is aware of the rock, to rocklike existence, which is unaware of the dog? Is it not therefore peculiar that God has been described solely in rocklike terms: pure actuality, permanence, only having external relations, unmoved, being and not becoming?

It might be wondered at this point why classical theism has been so popular among theists, in that it has so many defects. Hartshorne suggests at least four reasons, none of which establishes the case for classical theism: (1) It is simpler to accept monopolarity than dipolarity, that is, it is simpler to accept one and reject the other out of contrasting (or better stated, correlative, noninvidious) categories rather than to show how each, in its own appropriate fashion, applies to an aspect of the divine nature. Yet the simplicity of calling God "the absolute" can come back to haunt the classical theist if absoluteness precludes relativity in the sense of internal relatedness to the world.

(2) If the decision to accept monopolarity has been made, it is simpler to identify God as the absolute than to identify God as the most relative. Yet this does not deny divine relatedness, nor that God, who loves all, would therefore have to be related to all, or to use a roughly synonymous term, be relative to all. That is, God may well be the most relative of all as well as the most absolute of all, in the sense that, and to the extent that, both of these are excellences. Of course, God is absolute and is relative in different aspects of the divine nature.

(3) There are emotional considerations favoring divine permanence, as found in the longing to escape the risks and uncertainties of life. But even if these considerations obtain, they should not blind us to other emotional considerations, like those which give us the solace that comes from knowing that the outcome of our sufferings and volitions makes a difference in the divine life which, if it is all-loving, would certainly not be unmoved by the suffering of creatures, even nonhuman creatures.

(4) Monopolarity is seen as more easily made compatible with monotheism. But the innocent monotheistic contrast between the one and the many deals with God as an individual, not with the dogmatic claim that the divine individual itself cannot have parts or aspects or relatedness with the world.

In short, the divine being becomes, or the divine becoming is—God's being and becoming form a single reality:

> There is no law of logic against attributing contrasting predicates to the same individual, provided they apply to diverse aspects of this individual. (PS; 14–15)

The remedy for "ontolatry," the worship of being, is not the contrary pole, "gignolatry," the worship of becoming:

> God is neither being as contrasted to becoming nor becoming as contrasted to being; but categorically supreme becoming in which there is a factor of categorically supreme being, as contrasted to inferior becoming, in which there is inferior being. (PS; 24)

In process theism the divine becoming is more ultimate than the divine being only for the reason that it is more inclusive. (All of this should be kept before us when we look at Gunton's remarks.)

Hartshorne's theism is: (1) *dipolar* because excellences are found on both sides of these contrasting categories (that is, they are correlative, non-invidious); (2) a *neoclassical* theism because it relies on the belief that the classical theists (especially St. Anselm) were on the right track when they described God as the supremely excellent, all-worshipful, greatest conceivable being, but the classical theist did an insufficient job of thinking through the logic of perfection; (3) a *process* theism in that it sees the need for God to *become* in order for God to be called perfect, but not at the expense of God's always (that is, permanently) *being* greater than all others; and (4) a theism that can be called *panentheism,* which literally means "all in God"; God is neither completely ˙ removed from the world, that is, unmoved by it, as in classical theism, nor completely identified with the world, as in pantheism. Rather, God is: (a) world-inclusive in the sense that God cares for all the world; and all feelings in the world—especially suffering—are felt by God; and (b) transcendent in the sense that God is greater than any other being, especially because of God's love. Thus (IO; 366), Hartshorne rejects the conception of God as an unmoved mover not knowing the moving world (Aristotle); the unmoved mover inconsistently knowing the moving world (classical theism); and—contra Gunton—the conception of God as the unmoved mover knowing an ultimately unmoving, or at least noncontingent, world (Stoics, Spinoza, pantheism).

Two objections may be raised by the classical theist that ought to be considered. To the objection that, if God changed, God would not be perfect, for, if God were perfect, there would be no need to change, Hartshorne makes this rather obvious reply: in order to be supremely excellent God must at any particular time be the greatest conceivable being, the all-worshipful being. But at a later time, or in a situation where some creature that previously did not suffer now suffers, God has new opportunities to exhibit divine, supreme excellence. That is, God's perfection does not just allow God to change, but requires God to change.[3]

The other objection might be that God is neither one nor many, neither actual nor potential, and so forth, because no human concept whatsoever applies to God literally or univocally, but at most analogically. The classical theist would say, perhaps, that God is more unitary than unity, more actual than actuality as these are humanly known. Yet one wonders how the classical theists, once they have admitted the insufficiency of human conceptions, can legitimately give a favored status to one side (the left side) of conceptual contrasts at the expense of the other. Why, Hartshorne asks, if God is more simple than the one, is God not also more complex in terms of relatedness to diverse actual occasions than the many? Analogical predication and negative theology can just as easily fall victim to the monopolar prejudice as univocal predication. "To be agent and patient is in truth incomparably better than being either alone". (IO; 54) Hartshorne is quite clear on this point, Gunton's protests to the contrary. A human being is vastly more of an agent and patient than is an ape or a dog, which are more of both than a stone. Stones can neither talk nor listen, nor can they decide for others or appreciate others' decisions.

At this point one might wonder exactly what the issue is concerning Hartshorne's supposed disproportionate treatment of the two poles. Much of what is claimed in Hartshorne's dipolar theism is acceptable to Gunton, but he objects to what he thinks is the priority Hartshorne gives to terms listed above in the right-hand column, particularly passivity. What we have seen Hartshorne say above at the very least makes it easy to discredit Gunton's implied stance that Hartshorne always gives priority to one pole. But Gunton's position seems to be that even if Hartshorne claims some sort of polar equality in his dipolar theism, he cannot do so consistently.

Hartshorne admits that, in terms of concrete aspects, God is relative, contingent, passive, and so forth. This logical and ontological "priority" given to God's relativity, arrived at primarily on the evidence of Hartshorne's claim that divine becoming is more inclusive than divine being, makes the absolute, as Gunton sees it, an empty abstraction. God is absolute only because God is relative to the whole of reality, whereas other beings can have at best a limited relatedness to the world. God's all-embracing relativity is God's absoluteness. So also God's necessity solely consists in God's contingency, which would mean for Gunton that God always has the possibility for change; God's contingent existence must always be. God is eternal not by virtue of creating time but because God always exists in time; God's being consists merely in God's becoming. God "is" only in abstraction from the becoming that takes place in God. God is immutably mutable; divine immutability only consists in God's always being uniquely mutable.

All of this is what Gunton claims Hartshorne ought to hold. But why? Gunton does not have anything near the evidence from Hartshorne's texts that he needs to defend his thesis claiming an extreme polar inequality in Hartshorne's conception of God. He largely builds his case by looking through the aperture of one particular polar contrast: activity–passivity. But even though Gunton is weak on textual grounds, his thought experiment in process theology deserves a reply, if for no other reason than the fact that his view mirrors what many who have not read Hartshorne carefully assume he has said. And of those who have read Hartshorne carefully, some surprisingly defend Gunton, hence my citation of so many of Hartshorne's often-repeated remarks. We forget more than we remember.

That God is supremely passive, or supreme effect, Hartshorne would not deny. All that has happened or is happening is experienced by God; God is the whole of process to date. The question is: Can Hartshorne's God also be supremely active, or the supreme cause? Gunton thinks not. God's supreme pasivity makes God exclusively a God of the past and present in that it is only the past and present that have so far exerted an influence on God. God's causal "power" with respect to the future is of the weakest sort, that is, God's causation lacks agency. Hartshorne's God only acts as an abstract cause, a lure, like Aristotle's gods or Plato's form of the good (as opposed to Plato's World Soul or Demiurge).[4] Ironically, despite Hartshorne's intentions, he is accused of having returned to something similar to the abstract deity of classical theism, which Gunton would also like to criticize: rather than an unmoved mover Hartshorne has a moved unmover.

God's abstract causality can either be efficient, in the sense that the past contains the possibilities for future action, or final, in the sense of God acting as an ideal model. But both types of causality are merely abstract. Hartshorne has made God's activity into a mere divine map or statue. Using the list of polar opposites above, we can see activity, or cause, and abstraction on the same side. More than a visual connection is to be found here for Gunton because Hartshorne's God is essentially passive, that is, effect; God's causal power is an abstraction from God's passivity. For example, God listens to us and feels our sufferings and then, if we pay attention to God's loving passivity, we are "caused" to lead better lives in imitation of God. Gunton seems to ask: Is that all there is? The weaker is God's activity, the closer Hartshorne gets to Spinozistic or Eastern pantheism; and exclusively abstract activity is indeed weak.

An immediate response to Gunton might be: Even if the absolute is an abstraction, that does not mean God is an abstraction, since absoluteness is only one pole of God's nature, and is not to be identified with God. Hartshorne is not a Hegelian, nor a Spinozist, nor pantheist, as he makes abundantly clear (PS). And even if God does have abstract causality, that does not necessarily exhaust God's causal power. In addition to the points made above and in this preliminary response, the following three are also in order:

(1) Supposing Gunton to be correct that for Hartshorne, God is merely an abstract agent, it should be noted that it is no small feat to be an abstract cause of supreme excellence. Even St. Augustine would admit that God's full knowledge of the Platonic forms is significant, and unique to God. Nor is it a small accomplishment to act as a perfect lure or map. Good lures (or maps, as any traveller knows!) are hard to come by, perfect ones harder still. Now it must be admitted that the initial subjective aim of the universe provided by Whitehead's God has been trimmed somewhat by Hartshorne, who believes that only the *most* abstract possibilities are nonemergent and evidenced on

the divine map. These would include, I think, the structure of creativity itself, and the more formal properties in mathematics, among other things. But I think it is premature to conclude that God as a lure or map in Hartshorne is of no consequence. An example may help. It is much easier for us in the West to be moved religiously by a Crucifixion scene painted by one of the northern Renaissance masters than by the lines and shapes of Mondrian. Yet some might say that the terrible historical clarity of Western religious art could learn something from the complex geometrical patterns found in Islamic art, where art remains the felicitous handmaiden of the divine, rather than its master. Plato's treatment of art in the *Philebus* is instructive in this regard.

(2) But does God do anything else?, Gunton will ask. Yes. Disorder without limit would be unintelligible, severe disorder would be intelligible but ugly. Inflexible order may entice some, but divine decisions made in minute detail for creatures produce not beauty but monotony; chaos is avoided but freedom precluded, as we will see regarding Hartshorne's aesthetics of bird song. That is, what God does, according to Hartshorne, in addition to exerting divine abstract causality, is to limit disorder to such an extent that beauty and freedom are possible for creatures. As Hartshorne often says, some of us do not wish for more than that. Once again, *making* it possible for human beings (*and* other creatures) to be free is no small accomplishment. It should be emphasized that God's concrete reality, as can be seen in the dipolar list, is potential, and the future is the only region in which the potential can become actualized. God's freedom works against Gunton's belief that Hartshorne's God must be merely a God of the already actualized past and present. Becoming, change, and contingency are all fundamental features of God's concrete reality for Whitehead and Hartshorne, and these features presuppose the ability to act in some nonabstract way.

(3) Nevertheless, Gunton forces Hartshorne or his defenders to be more precise with respect to the active–passive contrast. Given Hartshorne's previously mentioned claim that passivity refers to the way in which an individual's activity takes account of, and renders itself appropriate to, the activities of others (PS; 2), one suspects that the need for a more precise use of language on Hartshorne's part is called for, otherwise the contrast will turn into an active–active redundancy. Let me make what I think are friendly amendments to Hartshorne's thought so as to defend him against Gunton's charges.

What Hartshorne is trying to do is incorporate excellent receptivity into the divine life, which classical theists still fail to do. The correlative to receptivity is not activity, for being excellently receptive *is* a type of activity. For example, one must work hard to listen to the argument of others, or sense their subtle pains, or hear the counterpoint in a difficult symphony. As Hartshorne makes clear, receptivity is passive *and* active. The correlative to excellent receptivity can perhaps best be described as excellent impassibility, as Gunton almost came to realize, in the sense that God prevents anything from happening which would stop God's excellent receptivity. Further, God acts abstractly as a lure for Hartshorne, but also concretely as a persuader, as in Whitehead. Excellent persuasion is active, but also passive because persuasion, as opposed to authoritarian dictation, is engaged in within the confines of a conversation where one must also listen. Dropping active–passive from the above list, we may refine the diagram by adding:

> impassibility receptivity (passive and active)
> lure   persuader (active and passive)

Gunton comes close at several places to points (1) and (2), and actually flirts with, but eventually rejects, what I suggest in point (3).[5] Yet he still persists in asking: Is that all there is to divine activity? I suspect that the reason for this is his own residual classical theistic prejudice regarding what meaningful divine activity is, although he would surely reject a designation as a classical theist. To use his own metaphors, he wants to hold out for a God who has the power and activity of a general over an army, the judiciary over a prisoner, or a lion over an antelope (pp. 44–46). But this falls precisely into the classical theist's trap, for generals and lions are not known for their receptivity, and courts are receptive only intermittently and imperfectly. No doubt Gunton would also like to say that such a God is a God of peace, which is analogous to the classical theist's inconsistent desire for a God of love who yet remains an unmoved mover. The fact that Gunton wants God to be like a general or to behave like a lion with an antelope makes one wonder if he has totally ignored the connection between classical theism, on the one hand, and militarism and ecological rapacity, on the other. God , unlike the lion, has no need to kill antelopes.

One is reminded here of Whitehead's famous lines in "Peace" from the very end of *Adventures of Ideas:*

> At the heart of the nature of things, there are always the dream of youth and the harvest of tragedy. The Adventure of the Universe starts with the dream and reaps tragic Beauty. This is the secret of the union of Zest with Peace:— That the suffering attains its end in a Harmony of Harmonies. The immediate experience of this Final Fact, with its union of Youth and Tragedy, is the sense of Peace. In this way the World receives its persuasion towards such perfections as are possible for its diverse individual occasions.

This is one of those profound passages that is perhaps best left on its own, but I cannot resist the temptation to emphasize that "the sense of Peace" consists in an *immediate* experience. Mediation through brute power always keeps us at least one additional step away from peaceful, Godlike becoming-being. But it is just such mediation that Gunton wants God to exhibit, as in the military and carnivore metaphors, which he takes rather seriously. The dipolar process theist need not consider it a defect if God does not act in this way.

In sum, there is dipolar equality in Hartshorne's theism because: (1) the abstractness of God as absolute cause is not to be identified with God, because God is also concrete; (2) even God's abstract causality is not to be denigrated, in that God is the only supremely excellent abstract cause; (3) God acts by concretely limiting disorder so as to avoid chaos, but not to the extent that such ordering leads to an aesthetic monotony or to the notorious problems surrounding the possibility of human freedom found in classical theism; (4) God acts so as to prevent anything from happening that would stop God's excellent receptivity; (5) God acts as both a lure and a persuader, with neither receptivity nor persuasion being purely passive;[6] and (6) God orders the world by giving free creatures an awareness, however dim, of their place in the cosmos.

What can be learned from Hartshorne is that we should look not so much at what God does *to* the universe (although God does create the cosmos *as* a cosmos), but at what God does *in* and *with* it: God cherishes it and the creatures in it, and makes them contributory to the divine life, such that ephemeral creatures acquire everlastingness; if God loves not only us but animals as well, neither we nor these creatures will be destroyed (GN; 58–59). As we shall see, however, if a world without creaturely freedom is not an option, not even for God (even if God can change laws of nature, which are also creations), then animals can be expected to be tragic beings. [7] The root of tragedy is the conflict of good with good (GN; 60), yet our solace can always be found in the realization that God alone appreciates every creaturely nuance. As Oliver Goldsmith expresses the issue in "The Hermit":

> No flocks that range the valley free
> To slaughter I condemn;
> Taught by the power that pities me,
> I learn to pity them.

Yet without the least taint of shrillness, the Nobel Prize winning author, Isaac Bashevis Singer, reminds us that the contemporary world has not been persuaded by Goldsmith's rhetoric: "for the animals it is an eternal Treblinka."

With all of these technical distinctions in Hartshorne's theory of God before us, we should now be in a position to see both how Hartshorne's theory of God avoids the vast chasm between Creator and creatures in classical theism while maintaining the traditional Western belief in a personal God who is that than which no greater can be conceived. Both of these features will come into play in the attempt to understand the metaphysical place of animals in the cosmos. That is, fair treatment of animals is an intimate part of the effort to develop a consistent generalization from the basis of theism.

For Hartshorne, the notion of a tyrannical God, albeit a supposedly benevolent one, cannot be logicaly defended. It follows from this thesis that human beings should not emulate the classical theistic God as tyrant by developing a fetish for coercive power over animals. "The ultimate power is the power of sensitivity," and "all power is sensitivity" (DR; 154–155). This marks a departure from classical theism in that divine power is, above all else, not reliant on "brute power" but on love. Brute power may well be, at times, an instance of sensitivity for diverse actual occasions, but on Hartshorne's grounds, only indirectly. Vegetarianism not only avoids the bastardized form of peace with animals which Whitehead might call "Anaesthesia," but has the advantage of being a more *direct* and a more powerful exhibition of sensitivity. Brute power over animals is more indirect than vegetarianism because it kills to affirm respect for animal life.

An eternal object or universal for Hartshorne is not a detached, static, pure form with a life of its own, which is then imitated by actual occasions or moments of experience in the world. The eternal object, "peace," enters into the real world only as a constitutive element in real becoming.[8] Nonviolence toward animals is a way of becoming, indeed specifically, a more direct way of becoming like the divine Becoming. The way the eternal object, "peace," enters into the real world partially depends on the subjective form of the prehending actual occasion that brings it into the real world. There can be diverse prehensions (or apprehensions) of the same eternal object. Vegetarianism is only one way in which peace with animals can be experienced, but the most appropriate way because of the great value intensity it yields. Philosophical vegetarianism is a disciplined attempt to attain what Whitehead in *Adventures of Ideas* calls "that Harmony of Harmonies which calms destructive turbulence and completes civilization."

Violence consists in determining other actual occasions through dominance. In place of a contrast yielding mutual satisfaction, there is conflict, a vying for control rather than creativity. Nonviolent actions alone preserve the desire to actualize the intrinsic value of every actual occasion. All of this is suggestive of God, one of whose contributions to the world for many process philosophers is the supply of its initial subjective aim. From the perspective of humanity, God's initial aim can be variously interpreted, but, for Hartshorne, God's way is typified by persuasion rather than coercion. As Whitehead put it, "God's role is not the combat of productive force with productive force, of destructive force with destructive force; it lies in the patient operation of the overpowering rationality of his conceptual harmonization." God does not desire, it is safe to say, the repetition of yesterday's violence.

Chapter Three

Commonality with Animals

> *No officious slave*
> *Art thou of that false secondary power*
> *By which we multiply distinctions, then*
> *Deem that our puny boundaries are things*
> *That we perceive, and not that we have made . . . .*
> *Let Nature be your teacher.*
> *Sweet is the Lore which Nature brings;*
> *Our meddling intellect*
> *Mis-shapes the beauteous forms of things*
> *We murder to dissect.*

    With the two preliminary chapters behind us (the first dealing with the understanding of animals in the world's great religions, the second with Hartshorne's notion of God), we are now in a position to view Hartshorne's thoughts on animals. Here in Chapter Three I will emphasize what we have in common with animals, and with higher animals in particular; this effort will also allow us to see what human beings have in common with the rest of contingent reality. As before, however, these commonalities do not preclude our being superior to animals in some ways, as most religions have indeed suggested. This will become obvious in Chapter Four, in which the theory of unity-in-difference with animals is completed.

    By "higher animals" Hartshorne refers to vertebrates. Any ethical relationships we have with invertebrates are not governed by additional principles, only by a diminished application of the principles that govern (or should govern) our relations with vertebrates. What do we have in common with the higher animals? Hartshorne's perhaps surprising response is "multicellular bodies," including complex nervous systems (FH; 154). Although the discovery of cells is three hundred years old, the idea of cells is still largely unassimilated in our general culture, particularly in ethics. An organ is a society of cells, with the body itself being a society of societies of cells. Each cell is an individual in a stronger sense than an organ is.

In that ethics is concerned with social relations, we should notice that our very bodies, and all animal bodies, are cases of social organization and cooperation. "If our cells were not unconsciously, instictively ethical . . . we could not be consciously so." All higher animals are examples of life's serving life. Nature is in some sense a single enterprise, although what this enterprise is may be difficult to determine. Two oversimplifications are to be avoided: (1) The notion that nature represents a war of all against all fails to do justice to the cooperation entailed in animal bodies themselves, not to mention solar systems. And (2), the classical theistic view that nature is the working out of a single, omnipotent purpose fails to account for much that goes on in the natural world, including earthquakes, as Candide found out when Pangloss explained them as evidence of this being the best of all possible worlds.

Animals are organized societies of individuals (FH; 155). They are different from plants in that they are also individuals as wholes. Here is where the nervous system is so important. Although plants and trees are multicellular organisms, they are many things taken as one, but they are not individuals in any deep sense. Lacking a nervous system, a tree's parts, like a forest's parts, are for the most part on their own. "To cut down a tree is not analogous to killing a deer or even a fish, but rather to destroying a colony of paramecia or bacteria." Although a tree is composed of cellular individuals, it is not an individual on the supercellular level, as will be seen. Plants do not thirst even though their cells need water. (CA; 129) Whitehead puts the point this way in *Science and the Modern World*:

> The concrete enduring entities are organisms, so that the plan of the *whole* influences the very characters of the various subordinate organisms which enter into it. In the case of an animal, the mental states enter into the plan of the total organism and thus modify the plans of the successive subordinate organisms until the ultimate smallest organisms, such as electrons, are reached. Thus an electron within a living body is different from an electron outside it. (EA; 163)

The nervous system is that subsociety of cells which makes human beings and higher animals supercellular individuals. In dreamless sleep we become, in a bastardized way, what we would be like without a nervous system: a mere colony of cells. As Aristotle put it: "A tree is like a sleeping man who never wakes up." Botanists explain growth in plants through cells, not nervous systems. And as Whitehead put it, "a tree is a deomcracy." (00; 79, 106)

Individuality at the supercellular level, or in the strong sense, is not just physiological, but psychological as well. Although physiological workings provide some objective evidence of individuality, individuality as such is psychical. To sum up, animals are sentient in two senses (FH; 156): (1) They are sentient at a microscopic level in the experiences of each concrete individual, which occur in plants and rocks as well. We shall call this Sentiency 1 (S1). (2) They have sentiency per se, which consists in those experiences, lapsing in dreamless sleep, that enable the animal as a whole to feel pain, or, at times, to remember or anticipate pain, that is, to suffer. This is Sentiency 2 (S2). In that S1 is sufficient to refute the materialist, but not sufficient to attribute pain or suffering to plants—where S2 is needed—plants can be eaten with equanimity, even if they too have some inherent value, whatever that means in this context, because of S1. Because plants never act as sentient individuals does not mean that, by way of contrast, animals always do. S2 lapses into dreamless sleep, just as S1 may lapse in a cell that only has unified experience at the moment when its membrane triggers an impulse. At other times the cell is an aggregate of subcellular individuals (EA; 182). It must be admitted that if we treat subcellular "entities," to be treated later, as individuals, and cells as aggregates of these, then the analogy between these subcellular individuals and the experiences of animals is weakened. That is, cells viewed as individuals provide a stronger analogy than subcellular individuals to human or animal experiences at a given moment.

We should object to unnecessary pain given to animals because *they* suffer, not simply because their cells suffer. The parts are for the whole, which is the opposite of our usual egalitarian view of politics, according to which the group is just a means of securing the welfare of the members. In an animal, however, the whole is also an individual, like the parts. By way of extension we can also note that for Hartshorne each individual animal (a part) seeks not only its own preservation and enhancement, but also its species' enhancement of nature as a whole—God. Individuality is indeed a difficult thing to explain, because it can mean so many things (FH; 157). In the long run *all* individuals and species are insignificant when compared to God, but in the short run our challenge is to avoid giving in to the temptation that suggests self-preservation as the first law of nature, thereby giving sanction to human egoism and mistreatment not only of other human beings, but of animals, perhaps especially animals, as well.

What makes an animal, even a human animal, the same individual? Once the terms "soul" and Aristotelian "substance" were combined in classical theism, an exaggerated metaphysical individualism invaded Western culture.

For Hartshorne, however, "being oneself" is at most a matter of degree, and not something absolute. On the bodily level only our nerve cells endure throughout life, which comes as a surprise to those who know little about physiology. Individuality is based on a pattern of interaction, not a physical or mental concrete stuff. That is, units of individual reality, or any reality for that matter, are neither physical nor mental substances. As Hartshorne puts it:

> The concrete units of reality are unit-processes, unit-events, singular cases of becoming or creation. Reality consists of actions, not things. What then acts? To ask this question is to attempt to force, in too crude a manner, the structure of language on that which language is about. (FH; 158)

From quantum mechanics comes the theory of identity, whereby an entity is determined by its relations with others rather than by the "stuff" which is its body. To conceive of reality in process terms enables one to intelligently respond to the problem of individual identity, concerning which there are three basic options (EA; 123): First, there is the strict identity view of Gottfried Leibniz, which relies on Aristotle, whereby a series of states mutually imply one another; in me at birth, incredibly enough, is my whole earthly career, including my death. This view spatializes time in a way anathema to everything Henri Bergson contributed to philosophy. The opposite view, held by David Hume and Bertrand Russell, has each successive state externally related to every other; it is also a symmetrical view, but one that, in effect, denies individual identity. Hartshorne's asymmetrical view allows us to make sense *both* of process and of individual identity: "states include and are constituted by predecessors but not by successors."

Hartshorne is among that minority of philosophers who are panpsychists, or as he calls them, psychicalists. He holds that anything concrete feels, leaving out of the picture abstractions like "blue" and collections of concrete individuals like "two cats," which may feel individually, but not collectively (CS; 141). Of course, tables do not feel, but that does not mean that there is no feeling within them. Although the table is "relatively concrete," it is really a collection of more concrete singulars: molecules, atoms, or, better, subatomic particles. As contemporary physics has made apparent, these concrete singulars do show signs of spontaneous activity and sensitivity to the environment around them; they are always in process. "Mere matter" construed as the "zero of feeling" and process, is an absolute negation whose meaning is wholly parasitic on what it denies (CS; 143). Nothing has ever been observed which logically could not exist with experience; even inert rocks have active atoms, molecules, or particles (CS; 160–161). Hartshorne holds, along with Leibniz, that no positive meaning can be given to the negative of "sentient" because all concrete things react to their environment (CS; 35, 112–113). If all concrete individuals are sentient, it might be asked if "sentient individual" loses its distinctive meaning. Not necessarily, because, as in the cases of tables or trees, many pseudo-individual entities are not really individuals at all. As Hartshorne tells us in *Beyond Humanism,* rocks as swarms are dead, as is a porterhouse steak.

The historical dualism of mind and matter mistook composites for singulars, and materialism "groundlessly" attributed the qualities of the apparent singulars (like rocks) to the unperceived real singulars. Leibniz, along with Plato, was one of the few philosophers who almost saw that the true singulars have internal power (IO; 91). Hartshorne even goes so far as to say that Leibniz's panpsychism was the greatest step in the second millenium of philosophy (MN; 95). In order to accurately describe these active units of process (Platonic self-movers), we must have recourse to the only active singulars we perceive as such: "ourselves, other animals" (IO; 131). Hartshorne returns to the Platonic and Leibnizian theme often: the principle of change or dynamic unity is psychical, in that a self-moving character, or "appetitive aspect," must be used to explain changes in each monad. Atoms or electrons do not push or pull, they repel or attract. "Methodological materialism" is still attractive. But when it is considered that universal psychicalism can account for the methodological appeal of materialism in the sciences (taking composites for singulars) as well as offering a more ultimate understanding of reality as a whole, its superiority becomes apparent (IO; 132–133).

As a working strategy of research, Hartshorne has no objections to a materialism that assumes no mental states and goes as far as it can on this parsimonious basis, but, as metaphysics, materialism would have a hard time refuting what Karl Popper and J. Z. Young have noticed: that in the amoeba there is a center of activity, exploration, and planning; and primitive choice can even be found in bacteria.[1] Or as David Bohm puts it, atomic events are internally related to other atomic events such that contemporary physics could not help but move away from the mechanistic approach that still dominates much of biology and psychology. An approach that only studies the mechanistic "explicate" order of things (that is, the exterior "objective" aspect of things) leaves unexamined the "implicate order" wherein microscopic "mentality" is evidenced in the ability to feel the difference between the past and the future. If we, as subjects, value our experiences *and hence* are of value, why not the same to a lesser degree with other subjects (especially animals with S2) with their own implicate order?

Ethics can in a certain light be seen as nothing other than the heightening of importance of internal relations.

If to be ethical means acting so as to maximize the intensity or importance of experience both for the occasions involved and for their descendants, then one can see the necessity for ethical ideals to be undergirded by instinctive and emotional depth. This need explains the slow rate of incorporation of ideals into custom and conduct, as is seen in Whitehead's discussion in *Adventures of Ideas* of the long history of the abolition of slavery, and in the even longer history of attempts to gain fair treatment for animals. That is, before fair treatment of animals is pervasive, human beings must *feel* their commonality with animals. As we will see, the obligations to maximize the significance of one's own experience as well as the experience of those within one's influence form the cornerstone of process ethics, which is superior on several grounds to other ethical views when animal rights and environmental ethics are considered.

It should not escape our notice that cost-benefit analysis and the short-term economic interests on which most decisions regarding animals and the environment are made are crude forms of utilitarianism. But even the sophisticated utilitarianism of Peter Singer, although it has played an incalculable role in bringing to light the preferences felt subjectively by individual animals, does not adequately treat the objective interconnections in an ecosystem or in a cosmos. Further, there is a difficulty concerning the grafting of self-consciousness and rationality onto sentience in utilitarianism that has consequences for the effort to delimit human transcendence of animality. Process philosophy's organic connectedness between desire and reason, feeling and self-consciousness, is a significant advantage in this regard. Self-consciousness "stems from sentience, but flowers into the awareness of alternatives." [2]

Process philosophy can also improve on Tom Regan's view that all subjects-of-a-life, which are inherently valuable, have an equality of inherent value. Regan's claim that subjects-of-a-life can be either moral agents or moral patients does a great deal to point out the commonality between human beings and animals in that both can be moral patients (for example, infants and frogs, the latter often viewed as mere objects for pithing). But Regan's notion that any doctrine of degrees of value would lead to an unjust subjugation of those possessing less value is not convincing, and for at least two reasons. First, it is not necessarily the case that a doctrine of degrees of value will lead to exploitation, although it must be admitted that often this occurs; and second, there are, as I shall propose in the next chapter, good reasons for believing that human beings have more inherent value than animals.

I shall further agrue that process philosophy can give sufficient emphasis to the notion of "moral patiency" so as to avoid exploitation of animals and still defend the idea of degrees of inherent value. Further, a Whiteheadian and Hartshornian approach, as we shall see, is in a better position to explain the aesthetic value of entities which are not subjects-of-a-life (for example, trees and rivers). A process approach would condem the destruction (or maiming) of any society of actual occasions unless such a society clearly threatened the intensity or satisifaction of a higher-order society. Hence a human being should—except in, say, extreme circumstances without vegetation nearby—subsist on plants because, although they have intrinsic value *in* them, their value is of a lower intensity and complexity than that in animals. And a human being can thrive on plant life and dairy products (in that these latter do not necessarily deprive animals of intrinsic value or cause them suffering).

Process ethics can also improve on the "land ethic" of Aldo Leopold, where the natural community of a given locale is the locus of value, as opposed to individual animals. That is, this conception deprives individuals of any value except as they contribute to the biotic community (hence Regan's charge of "environmental fascism"); and it grants no additional value to rationality or even to sentiency except as they might contribute to the community. As I stated earlier, Hartshorne's thought can provide all the respect due to individuals (hence it can incorporate the best insights of Singer and Regan) and still do justice to ecosystems, even to the cosmos as a whole when conceived as an animate community (God). From Chapter Two it should also be clear that Hartshorne can improve on the use of Spinoza as an ecologist, because Spinoza's view does not allow for evolutionary development, and is connected with deterministic monism, hence allows for no novelty in the world and no individual responsibility. For Hartshorne, the opposite is the case: The modes in process are ultimately real, not the "One."

I will now return to materialism, which was my object of concern before the above prolegomena to my ethical position, to be found in Chapter Five. Because materialism can be tolerated as a strategy of research, Hartshorne must admit that the advantages of psychicalism are metaphysical and ethical: (1) We can get rid of the problem of how lifeless matter could produce life, (2) We can do justice to the relative difference between life and "lifeless matter." That is, the word "sentient" does not lose its distinctive meaning, in that two contrasts still remain: between active singulars and inactive aggregates, and between low senient activity (S1) and high sentient activity (S2 or what I will later label S3), (3) Hume's problem of causality can be avoided, in that events are internally connected to previous events through concepts like memory and perception—the latter being a specific type of memory which appears to take place "instantaneously", (4) It can be shown how mind and body are related in animals. Pain is due to damaged cells; we participate in their suffering. Mind is found on both sides of the relation, but on different levles; the gap is crossed by sympathy. As is argued elsewhere, our cells can enjoy themselves or suffer. So it should not be surprising that Hartshorne suggests that sympathy can occur in the reverse direction as well, although cells cannot be as much aware of us as we are of them, (5) It can be shown that the traditional primary qualities (for example, extension) are causal-geometrical relationships, whereas secondary qualities (for example, the sensation of heat) are more concrete and are found in all active singulars along with tertiary (for example, pain) or value qualities. (MN; 92-93, 95)

The nineteenth-century German thinker, G. T. Fechner, expanded on Leibniz by distinguishing two different sorts of psychicalism—monadological and synecological—which are analogous to what I have designated as S1 and S2. Hartshorne rightly notes that the dynamic unity of action in a tree or plant is either nonexistent or too slight to justify Fechner's attribution of synecological psychicalism to them (IO; 248), although there is obviously striving *in* plants, even if they do not experience pleasure and pain as wholes (IO; 249). We should not be too harsh on Fechner's overly romantic view of trees, in that the pathetic fallacy is no less dangerous than the "prosaic" or "apathetic" fallacy, its opposite. "Reality is not as dull as many sober souls imagine" (IO;250). That is, the admission of contingency and partial disorder into concrete singulars removes the artificialities that precluded appreciation of Leibniz for two centuries (IO; 319).

The actual things in the world are careers, "world lines," or, as Whitehead put it, series of actual occasions. The primary concrete entities are happenings, unit cases of becoming or activity (FH; 159). Because none of these events in process are *completely* determined by antecedent conditions, which would end change in all its forms, creativity is a universal principle for Hartshorne. A feeling (of a microscopic event or by an animal individual) reacts to prior feelings, but it is also spontaneous, in however slight a way. Hartshorne and Whitehead oppose those "neat and tidy minds" who claim that indeterminacy is our lack of knowledge; in fact, it seems that when quantum physics in its present form is superceded (despite Einstein's "hopes" for determinism) we will move even further away from classical conceptions of substance, determinism, or insentient matter. It is not only human beings, nor only animals, that defy an absolute regularity in their actions (although statistical regularity may be present, distorted as it is by our observation of it). Even the very atoms defy such absolute regularity, as any student of contemporary physics knows. One of the objections Hartshorne has with the positions he opposes (materialism, determinism, atheism) is that they are purely negative or derivative (respectively denying experience, creativity, and unsurpassable experience and creativity) (EA; 6). From Erwin Schroedinger we can learn that it is observation of bodies (or better, waves or wave pockets) that puts a system into one state or another. The probability associated with a state is the probability that an observation or interaction will throw the system into that state. As before, an entity's identity is derived from its relations with others.

An atom is not just smaller than a table (or a mammal), it is a different kind of thing. We should all be materialists, *if* what is meant by "materialism" is that human beings and everything else are made up of smaller integrated units of actuality: molecules, atoms, atomic particles, or plant and animal cells (IO; 222–223). But this is not what is usually meant by the term; it usually means belief in inert lifeless stuff as the building blocks of the world. It is only a short step from this belief to the widely shared view that nature is "mere resource" for human exploitation. William James did not commit himself to panpsychism, although it appealed to him, because it did not appear pragmatically significant to characterize the nonhuman in positive terms. It is to be hoped that animal suffering and the current ecological crisis at least make obvious the pragmatic significance of the psychicalist position (PS; 336). Dualism can also easily lead to the view that nature is there for us to plunder, in that reality is mostly mindless, except for a few minds here and there that deserve consideration:

> The clearest basis for respect for nature is to renounce two forms of dualism: an absolute difference between matter and mind, and a quasi-absolute difference between the human and other forms of mind. (IO; 225)

For Hartshorne, the difference between materialsim and dualism is more verbal than real, and hylozoism was a more reasonable starting point than either of these views. That is, the psychical is not an addition to matter but the whole of what matter is (WM; 21, 115, 121).

Nonetheless, animals, whose experiences are true singulars, at least at a given moment (IO; 275), indicate that there *are* differences in nature, in that the "experiences" of composites like geraniums are not perceived as singulars. Only what acts as one also feels as one (GN; 62). But because of monadological psychicalism (S1), even in rocks and plants, absolute differences cannot be found:

> The fallacy of composition would be committed in inferring the sentience
> of stones from that of molecules, and the fallacy of division prohibits us from
> inferring the insentience or inactivity of molecules from that of stones.
> (IO; 294-295)

The atoms-to-rocks move is illustrated well in electromagnetic theory,
where electric fields of charged particles overlap-add-cancel so as to create fields
that can be described without reference to individual forces exerted by particles.
The big picture looks much different from its parts. Yet think of Jesus' remark
to the Pharisees, when they told him to silence his disciples, to the effect that
if they were to keep silence even the very stones would cry out (Luke 19:28–40).
In short, Hartshorne's psychicalism is opposed to materialism, to dualism (in
its various forms: experience versus nonexperience, mind versus matter, sentience
versus insentience—EA; 125), to idealism (if by idealism is meant that to be
is to be perceived by a *human* mind), and to emergence theory (which is, in
temporal respects, a dualism consisting of mindless matter first, then minded
matter—IO;343). Only from feeling can feeling come (GN; 61); this is far more
reasonable than the suggestion that from no feeling can arise feeling. And deity
synthesizes all feelings. Hartshorne is also obviously opposed to what Whitehead
calls the "fallacy of misplaced concreteness," that is, taking abstract composites
for concrete singulars.

What then do human beings have in common with the higher animals
that they do not have in common with atoms, rocks, and plants? S2 (or
synecological sentience) has already been cited; it is this which primarily
distinguishes the higher animals, including human beings, from other forms
of creation. Our species is a recent branch on a "tree of life" millions of years
old; countless steps led to the development of the nervous system and its
fruition—the brain. These we share with higher animals. In addition, the parti-
cularities of our neural structure we share with primates, whales, porpoises,
wolves, horses, cows, pigs, chickens, elephants. To assume that all of this development over so many years is mere preparation for human beings, although it
may *also* be just that, is to "exchange a sublime and coherent vision for a
childishly arbitrary one" (RS; 51). Arbitrariness is one of the hallmarks of
anthropocentric speciesism.

Hartshorne himself, however, advocates a "cautiously positive form of
anthropomorphism" (RS; 52). We should attribute to other creatures neither
the duplication of, nor the total absence of, those properties exhibited in high
degree, and in a refined or complex way, in us. Primitive animism is defective
in many ways, but it is nonetheless more reasonable than a view of the world

inherited from seventeenth-, eighteenth-, and nineteenth-century science: that the world is a machine "whose parts are submachines" (RS; 53). For Hartshorne, machines only occur when animals, especially human beings, make them. As Popper puts it, it is probably more accurate to say that clocks (symbols for absolutely determined regularity) are clouds (symbols for indeterminate reality exhibiting only statistical patterns) than it is to say that clouds are clocks. Not even machines are mere machines in their microscopic parts.[3]

For Hartshorne it is obvious that nature is there with or without us (pace Popper)—he is an epistemological realist but a metaphysical idealist. Yet we have no alternative to interpreting nonhuman nature by analogy with human nature. Our own natures are for us "the basic samples of reality" (IO; xiii).[4] Dialectic takes us *to* nonhuman nature, even if we can never have concrete nonhuman feelings. Perhaps God can, as we shall see later (IO; 198).

There are many examples of the analogy between animals and human beings. Mortality is an important one—there is no possibility of either animals or human beings not dying (IO; 52). Disanalogies also abound, as will be discussed in the next chapter. But not all of these disanalogies are due, as some may suppose, to human superiority; for example, we are partly color-blind in comparison to bees (IO; 294). The riddle is to try to know, or at least imagine, "how it feels to be another subject of feeling than one's own present self" (IO; 347). This is often difficult even with respect to one's own past selves, say, as an infant. Because of their simplicity, chimpanzees make the project easier, strange as that may seem; but because of their vastly different life styles, whales are much harder. Fish and insects are harder still; the hardest of all are paramecia, molecules, atoms, or particles. There is no need to try for clouds, winds, rocks, oceans, or perhaps even plants, for these are swarms or colonies of individuals, rather than true individuals.

God is also hard to imagine, but by no means impossible; even classical theists admit this much. Before human beings evolved on earth, prehuman animals experienced something of the world; before them plant cells had their minute experiences; before them molecules and atoms had their still more primitive analogues; only God at all times experienced all worldly actualities (IO; 353).

The basic principle human beings must use when trying to understand others—God or animals—is to analogize with what we know ourselves to be (GN; 61). (It should be noted, however, that it is only the concrete aspects of the divine actuality that need to be described analogically, for Hartshorne. God's abstract aspects—for example, the bare fact of God's existence rather than *how* God exists—can be described univocally: WM; 132). A reasonable

anthropomorphism can move cautiously upward to more exalted and universally efficacious mind and downward to lesser minds. In fact, Hartshorne tries
to avoid what he believes is a vicious type of glorification of animals which calls
animal self-centeredness rationality (IS; 82).

By trying to understand psychicalism we may notice what should be, but
often is not, right before our eyes:

> Although we do not know that there is such a thing as a mere machine, we
> do know that there are animals, creatures whose actions are at least altogether
> *as if* they were influenced by feelings, desires, hopes, fears, likes and dislikes,
> memories and expectations. We know, too, that in animals the principle of
> spontaneous motion, what Plato called the "self-motion" of soul, is normally
> apparent. (RS; 53)[5]

Materialism dies hard, however.[6] There are those who wish to preserve the belief
that certain Greeks (not Plato) had: that reality is made of bits of stuff,
substances. Hartshorne's view, on the other hand, is that every singular active
agent—there are no singular inactive ones, the seemingly inactive being
composites of active agents—resembles an animal in having some initiative
in its activity, or spontaneous movement, or feeling. The feelings of cells would
include their internal relationships and the stimuli they receive from other
cells—or in nerve cells, across synaptic connections. We have direct evidence
that cells do feel, that is, we feel pain because cellular harm is done. Our suffering is an immediate sharing in, or sympathy with, feeling in our cells.
Granted, awareness of our cells is blurred, in that we cannot identify the microindividuals as such, but our experience of pain indicates cellular feeling
nonetheless. (OO; 61)

Not only do we share in, or have sympathy with, feelings in our cells,
we also, in a way, feel our own past feelings and sympathetically imagine our
future feelings. Similar relations to the past or future feelings of others explain
the possibility of altruism. The question regarding our relations with animals
often is: How far are we willing to generalize the scope of our sympathy at a
given moment for life at other moments? That is, both self-concern and other-
concern are forms of one principle—sympathy—which is neither substantial
identity nor simple nonidentity. "Compassion is a metaphysical truth, not
merely a psychological achievement."[7] As living animals, we integrate our cells,
whatever our psychological disposition, and there is no agent in a moment of
experience doing the integration. Rather, the occasion is the arising of a new
integration, which is the emergent entity. Notice that pain is localized (although

unhappiness is not), as when I stub my toe; so is pleasure localized, as in sex. And where there is feeling, there is valuing or mattering, and in more than an instrumental sense:

> All nature involves self-enjoyment and contributes thereby to the participatory enjoyment of deity, which contribution is the absolute and final measure of its degree of importance. (RS; 54)

The greatest conceivable being *cares* for all. But once again, this is not a night in which all cows are black. Important distinctions among the different sorts of sentient reality can be made. Mountains, trees, vegetables, and rivers feel, or better, have feeling *in* them, but they are composites of active singulars. Only their invisibly small constituents have a remote analogy to our own inner life and activity.

Hartshorne's distinction between human beings and animals, on the one hand, and plants, on the other, seems to agree with Whitehead's view of things.[8] Each living body for Whitehead is a society of actual occasions, but "most of the animals, including all of the vertebrates, seem to have their social system dominated by a subordinate society which is 'personal'." A personal society of presiding occasions—called a dominant monad by Leibniz—(MN; 66) is purely temporal; hence in one sense a dog is a personally ordered society when "the genetic relatedness of its members orders these members 'serially'." Obviously, in stronger senses of the term "person," which depend on the heights of human mentality, a dog is not a person (as we will see in Chapter Four), nor is a mentally enfeebled human being. (WM; 32)

For Whitehead there are differences among the intensity levels in different entities, hence there are gradations in their determination or satisfaction. The problem for "Nature" is to produce societies that have a high degree of complexity but that are not highly specialized; thus intensity can be mated with survival. Crystals and rocks survive, but they are not intense. They are the lowest grade of structured societies in that there is an elimination of diversity among members; hence we call these societies "inorganic." In structured societies that are living or organic we find the origination of conceptual novelty on a societal level. Even the cell is such a society, indeed it is like an "animal body" in that it is composed of subservient inorganic societies in which there is no unified mentality guided by an inherited past in *each* of its occasions.

Endurance (or efficient causality) binds an occasion to its physical ancestry while life (or final causality) requires novelty, a clutching at vivid immediacy. (And as we shall see in Chapter Five, this life demands food, which requires a "robbery" in need of "justification.") Although molecules within an animal body exhibit peculiarities not noticed outside an animal body, it is only persons (including some higher animals) who can have hybrid prehensions of eternal objects, that is, a grasp of universals. Even human persons, however, have many bodily actions that are not completely under unifying control, for example, localized pleasure and pain or a beating heart. Worms and jellyfish are extreme examples of decentralized, democratic animal societies, but even persons with conceptual prehensions and a richness of inheritance with a presiding occasion are a little like worms in that their personal dominance is always only partial.

Creativity is Whitehead's and Hartshorne's name for the ultimate principle by which the many things become one actual occasion; an actual occasion is a novel entity at least partially because it is different from any one of the many it unifies. Actual occasions incorporate the world into themselves by means of prehensions or feelings. The expansive use of experience or feeling in Whitehead and Hartshorne allows them both to make sense of the emergence of self-conscious experience out of the physical world and to assert that each individual has intrinsic value because it experiences its own existence. Hence Whitehead's claim that "we have no right to deface the value-experience which is the very essence of the universe."[9]

It is important to note, however, that there is no incompatibility between a doctrine of heirarchy of value, on the one hand, and noticing human commonality with animals, on the other. Consider that a nexus, for Whitehead, is a group of actual occasions (for example, oxygen, minerals, etc.); a society is a nexus with a social order (for example, "nonliving" societies such as sticks and stones as well as living societies); and personally ordered societies are societies that are serially related, where there is a single line of inheritance. Despite this hierarchy of value intensity there is commonality with animals because they, along with human beings, are at least living societies of actual occasions, if not personally ordered societies.

To say that animals are capable of a personal order is to suggest that they have a persistence of psychological traits and that they have a dominant or presiding occasion, a mind that inherits from all the subsocieties in the body in such a way that an intense experience can be produced from the integration of cellular data. As Susan Armstrong-Buck puts it:

> A dog, then, would be understood as an almost unimaginably complex entity made up of societies and nexūs with many sub-societies or actual occasions, culminating in a personally ordered society of dominant occasions. This society constitutes the psyche of the dog . . . . The differences then between

inorganic material and the highest reaches of human consciousness are due to differences in the organization of the constituent actual occasions into nexūs and structured societies. A conscious thought entertained by the dominant occasion of a human psyche is dimly foreshadowed by the conceptual prehensions of the simplest actual occasions in a piece of iron ore, tradition-bound though they are.[10]

No doubt Whitehead and Hartshorne would agree:

Without doubt the higher animals entertain notions, hopes, and fears. And yet they lack civilization by reason of the deficient generality of their mental functioning. Their love, their devotion, their beauty of performance, rightly claim our love and our tenderness in return. Civilization is more than all these; and in moral worth it can be less than all these.[11]

If the point to life in general, apart from civilized life, is to attain intense, novel, complex, and harmonious experiences (which are often in conflict) for creatures, especially animals and human beings, then God is needed. God functions in part as a model or as a persuasive impetus to exist as intensely, creatively, richly, and harmoniously as possible.

That there are laws of nature is providential, for the theist, in order to set limits to freedom—hence evolution presupposes God (OO; 71). Some new modes of behavior prove to be adaptive such that even entire species may change considerably, especially gregarious species like barn swallows. But the greater becomes the power of thinking, the more likely individual variety in behavior will be evidenced, even to the point of exterminating species symbiotically valuable to one's own species (OO; 84-85). (However, there are even subtle differences among individual singers within bird species—WM; 115.) This is the price one may have to pay in a universe without a tyrant as the idea of divine power, which would be far worse.

The less-than-sanguine features of freedom can be overemphasized, however. Symbiosis is far more prevalent: insects and birds help plants propagate, and plants help birds in various ways. Only believing in God as omnipotent tyrant creates the nasty problem of evil when freedoms collide (OO; 87-89). Animals largely serve the needs of their species through both instinct and culture, the latter of which is increasingly important in higher animals. Conflict and suffering cannot be wholly excluded; such is the price of diversity, which itself is partially constitutive of beauty, as we will see in Chapter Eight. And on lower levels of reality such conflict involves no wickedness (OO; 127).

Our best clues as to what is happiness conflict with the notion of "absolute" happiness, because there are incompatible desires, especially in the higher animals, who are capable of complex desires, hence complex frustrations (PS;10). All animals die, although only human beings know this (OO; 32, 47).[12] Yet only some human beings consider that the result of death is not chaos, but simply a return to the more pervasive type of order expressive of the world (OO; 134).

These last several paragraphs have indiciated, sometimes in Whitehead's cumbersome language, the transition to Chapter Four. This chapter will return, I hope, to Hartshorne's typical clarity. We move from noting the similarities between human beings and animals to noting their differences.

Chapter Four

Human Transcendence of Animality

So build we up the Being that we are;
Thus deeply drinking-in the soul of things
We shall be wise perforce . . . .
God . . . for our wants provides
By higher, sometimes humbler, guides,
When lights of reason fail . . . .
To every Form of being is assigned . . .
An active principle.

It is quite legitimate for human beings to emphasize their superiority to other animals, at least if such emphasis is within an overall field where it is realized that human beings themselves are animals. After considering human transcendence of animality here in Chapter Four, I will be in a position to balance this transcendence against the dominant theme of human commonality with animals in Chapter Three. This balance will provide me a proper fulcrum from which to consider ethical issues concerning animals in Chapter Five.

Dogs think doggishly. For all we know, however, dogs do not know this. Human beings are just as much prisoners of their own nature as dogs, but some human beings know this. "To know a mental limit as such is to be, in some sense and degree, beyond that limit" (CM; 208). It is in this way that human beings partially transcend their animality. The key question is: To what degree can such transcendence occur?

Human beings are the only animals that survey the animal kingdom, and their place in that "kingdom." Human beings are the only animals that survey the vegetable and mineral worlds and their place in the general scheme of things. Human beings are the only animals that can view the entire world as only an arbitrary, possible world. These enormous powers make it easy for some to suppose that they can completely escape all anthropomorphic limits, and even escape animality itself. To Hartshorne, it is obvious that this is impossible.

The distinction between human beings and animals is not due to their finitude and our being infinite; nor that we can know something about God, whereas animals have no sense of God whatsoever. Rather, the distinction is due to the fact that we enjoy the conscious understanding of our finitude (OO; 48). Because of this understanding we can compare ourselves to our former selves a year ago, plan for the future, and imagine how our lives will be preserved by God after death. Although we are not absolutely superior to animals, our relative superiority is nonetheless immense, as is evidenced by our poetry, which animals have never written. Birds do make music, however, as do gibbons, whales, insects, frogs, and lizards. But our music is not only more complex, in that we also resort to fairy tales to enhance it. Champanzees know a great deal about the world, but they are not scientists (OO; 48-49). Apes and porpoises experience the world temporally, and they can remember, if memory is the taking of past events into account in the present, but they cannot think about "all time and existence" (OO; 76; MN; 94). Animals communicate, but only human beings have *logos*, in the sense of "word" or "reason" (OO; 100). One must trace humanity back to its fetal origins to find innocence comparable to that in animals; not even infancy goes back far enough, as St. Augustine might agree (OO; 102-103). A three-year-old is already beyond the mental level of one of the great apes (OO; 112).

But our distinctiveness is not necessarily tied to our egocentricity; even animals can perceive themselves "here," everything else "there." We are different in that we *know* we are egocentric, and we know, or should know, that egocentricity is an illusion (OO; 124). We can even imagine what it would be like to be God, to the point where we might deceive ourselves into thinking we were not creatures at all; we can "play God." This seems to be due to our symbolic power; only we can make sophisticated maps, diagrams, paintings, musical notations. (OO; 129-130)

Animal limitations affect human beings. For example, human beings perceive from a spatio-temporal perspective. Human beings are always here and now, "while most of the world is there and then." All animals, as animals, are severely limited in this way. Even for human beings *concrete* reality is only fractionally knowable. (CM; 209) Regarding our human past, for example, it is extremely difficult to even know how small the fraction is. This is what makes *abstract* reality so appealing; knowledge of it convices us of our transcendence. While scientific experiments only allow us to know about how nature operates in our own cosmic epoch, abstract thought gives us courage to speculate about what is *always* the case. Such thought is usually called "metaphysics" by philosophers, and consists not in a "probability estimate based on supposedly fair samples" (CM; 210), but on logical truths which, if they hold at all, hold in all possible conditions; their denial is not false, but impossible (CM; 211).

For example, absolute indeterminism does not make sense for an animal. To hold that, no matter what has happened up to now, anything may happen next with equal probability denies the fact that just to live from moment to moment is to face the future in terms of the past (CM; 212). Events have to be followed by at least some other events causally congruent with them, although not necessarily by the precise events that do follow. Animals know that the past discloses some information about the future (CA; 151, 178), that is, memory is not just human.

The metaphysical issue regarding freedom is: What is the extent of determination placed on animals? Animals in process constantly add definiteness, further specificity, to their lives. *Grasping* this abstract idea allows human beings to transcend those other animals, although they also substitute "determinates" for "determinables," just human beings do (CM;212-213). The unique capacity to know strictly universal or necessary truth is connected with human language and symbolism.

If a dog's whimpering and clawing at the door cannot inform one of the animal's need to go out, then neither can the student's verbal and plaintive request that he has to go the bathroom. In fact, the student may be lying. That is, the difference betwen natural bearers of meaning (animals) and conventional bearers of meaning (humans) is largely a matter of degree. For example, many, if not most, of the attributions of pain we make to other human beings are not based on articulated evidence, but on their writhings, the sight of blood, etc., all of which are exhibited by the higher animals.[1] Animals cannot speak in abstractions, nor about universal or necessary truth. This has led those who are a bit too hasty to assume that the difference between animal communication and human communication is a matter of kind, not degree. There is an analogy between sign language used by the deaf and some communication systems that the great apes can learn. Although human superiority is evident, it is not absolute; and we are in no position yet to state what communication and thinking whales and dolphins are capable of (IO; 226). From all we know now, however, because animals lack high-level linguistic and sign usage, they are incapable of explicit awareness of awareness, or rather reflexive awareness (IO; 278).

We do not know what it would be like to be, and hence exclusively communicate like, a gorilla, a turtle, a bee. We can observe these creatures, and empathize with them when they do communicate to us their feelings. But what is it like to *be* them, or, better, *become* like them? Only God knows, and this is to be taken literally:

> If there is any content to the idea of God, it should, I hold, include the notion of a form of experience or knowledge for which it is possible to know what each and every creature is like in and for itself. (CM; 213)

Although we may, in a way, transcend animals, this transcendence is not sufficient to support the case (implied in many of our dealings with animals, particularly eating them) for an anthropocentric universe. For practical purposes, we must treat stones as if they have no feeling in them, and the same at times for lions, but this does not establish the case that lions are different in kind from us. The vast differences in degree between human beings and animals are sufficient to support the humane moral and political purposes most of us would defend, for example, human rights. To say that normal adults have rights in the strongest sense, however, does not preclude the possibility that animals, subnormal adults, and infants have them in a weaker sense (CA; 232-234). Here Hartshorne obliquely defends the argument from marginal cases, discussed in Chapter One.

To some extent we can anticipate how animals will behave, and we can even be reasonably sure that song birds enjoy their songs. But we do not know what avian enjoyment is qualitatively. (CM; 214) Although we can reduce the difference between bird thoughts and our own if we try, we can never know precisely what the remaining gulf between us and another form of life, animals or God, is. This largely explains the medieval fascination with angels, which allowed human beings to know something about God and themselves by considering beings slightly different from (and a little higher than) human beings.[2] I am suggesting that a contemporary study of animals can also allow us to discover both the strengths and weaknesses of *human*ism. We do know that animals have feelings, both because we ourselves have feelings and because an animal's internal bodily structure (especially its nervous system) and behavior are similar to ours when we feel (CA; 234). So in very *abstract* terms language can formulate the alternatives regarding the differences among animals, human beings, angels (if there are such), and God. In this knowledge our animality is left behind. *Concrete* knowledge of all the contingencies surrounding an animal's existence only exists in God, as an addition to God's formal essence. (CM; 215; CA; 142)

Of course, this knowledge that God has is not a necessary consequence of God's essence; if it were, there would be no freedom or contingency anywhere.

"Freedom is contingent self-making, and causality is simply the influence of antecedent acts of self-making upon subsequent acts" (CM; 215).

Although it is hard for creatures (even human creatures) to know how much creativity they have, they most definitely have it. "Causal regularities mean not the absence of open possibilities, but their confinement within limits" (CM; 216). Just as the banks of a river determine where the water will go (ignoring floods), although leaving open an almost infinite number of possibilities for each drop of water, so also causal regularities regulate creaturely freedom. The complete determinist would have to reduce the possible channels between the banks to zero, but he would thereby eliminate the river altogether. Likewise, to eliminate creative process altogether is to eliminate life.

The medieval schoolmen helped to clarify the difference between the "categories" applicable to all creatures and the "transcendentals" applicable to creatures and their creator. For process philosophers, *the* transcendental is creativity, or in other words, response to previous instances of response. God is the unsurpassable form of creativity (or better, surpassable only by this very form in one of its subsequent phases); creatures are surpassable forms of creativity (IO; 78). A reasonable indeterminism holds:

> not that some concrete events "have no causes," but that the *exact* nature of ensuing events is left unspecified by the totality of their causal conditions. Something is left for the momentary self-determination of events. (IO; 141)

When an animal eats, it transforms what is eaten into uncreative flesh and blood; but the most concrete realities are not things like flesh and blood, but "momentary instances of creativity" (IO; 199). Even Kierkegaard shows his classical theistic roots in thinking that freedom or creativity is human or divine, but not both. If nonhuman creatures are not free in any sense, then the contingency necessary for change to occur must be viewed simply as divine freedom. That God is our creative ground "does not distinguish us from other animals" (IO; 213, 229), for pragmatic as well as other reasons:

> Every animal must act as if the future were partly forseeable from past experience; but no animal need, and none, strictly speaking, could, act as if the future in concrete details were absolutely, completely foreseeable from the past. Such absoluteness has no pragmatic meaning. (IO; 302)

That is, every animal in a sense knows that the world is ordered, but no animal could know (or wish to know!) that the world is absolutely ordered, for such knowledge would prevent it from acting. It is impossible in principle to predict the *details* of animal behavior (MN; 92). "Metaphysics is the search for the most universal of the vital truths by which animals unconsciously live" (IO; 374). Human beings are the animals who are born not knowing much how to live, but our ape-like consciousness, along with our unique capacity for intensive use of symbols, does catch glimpses of necessary truths, making us vicarious spectators of all existence (IO; 378-379).

Human beings always remain human beings, a kind of animal:

> Man can know enough to know that he has reason to be humble, not so much because others may be better than he, as because he himself is at every moment tempted to betray the only ideal which can withstand all criticism, the ideal of valuing other individuals . . . or of helping others. (CM; 217)

These others include animals. In facing the concrete, a human being is never more than a gifted, thinking animal. In facing the abstract, however, a human being can have aspects of an identity with deity. Ethics and religion are essentially about abstract, superanimal ideals:

> It is the capacity for generality which is one with the capacity to employ symbols comparable to linguistic signs that makes man unique and preeminent among earth's creatures and enables him, in one aspect, to have partnership with deity. (CM; 217)

It should also be noted that human efforts at anthropomorphizing God can be read the other way around: there is something deimorphic about human beings (our relatively advanced forms of creativity), which is unfortunately what makes our exploitation of other animals possible (EA; 38). Although the difference between human and animal communicative and symbolic capacities is one of degree, it is a difference in degree so vast that for "many purposes one can safely forget that it is one of degree" (FH; 160).

The connection between our symbolic power and our unique type of freedom is found in the reflexive character of the former. If other animals talk, it seems to be about things other than talk. We talk about talk, we have the word "word." (FH; 161; MN; 90) The greater our power to generalize, and the greater our ability to be aware that we are generalizing, "the greater the range of options we can entertain for carrying out our purposes" (FH; 161–162). For example, we know that the concept "protein" is a necessary element in our diet; yet upon reflection we can see we are free to consider meat, fish, or vegetables to fulfill this need. "The use of symbols enormously expands the power to envisage universals as such" (FH; 162). There are necessary conditions in the past for human beings and the higher animals, but sufficient conditions "only for a considerable range of possibilities within which each decision maker finally determines what precisely and concretely happens" (OO; 17).

Every animal has something like the generalization "edible stuff." A fox may chase a rabbit or search for field mice; it will not eat bark off a tree. This calls into question the dogma that without human language animals can have no freedom whatsoever. Hartshorne admits, however, that without a system of abstract symbols this freedom is narrowly limited. Only a human being can decide to go on a hunger strike, choose to become a vegetarian, or make up his mind to ignore arguments for vegetarianism. Unfortunately, many human beings choose this last course, or at least choose not to choose to eat in a way different from their parents. I will return to vegetarianism in the next chapter.

One of the most remarkable "leaps in the dark" in the history of ideas is committed by those who say that a human being's career from birth to death is entirely determined or predetermined (by God). What makes this leap remarkable is that it is done in the face of a human being's enormous power to talk about and envisage possibilities (FH; 162). By some criteria, perhaps divine, even human freedom is slight, animal freedom even slighter. But the fact that the rivers may be narrow does not mean that their banks are at no distance from each other. Each moment of life is creative, in some slight way, in that at each moment the formless acquires form, the indeterminate acquires determinacy. Thus, each creature is also a creator, humbly sharing creativity with God. Human beings enact "the transition from the nebulousness of possibility to the definiteness of actuality" (FH; 162-163) to a far higher degree than the other animals (not to mention plants or atoms). To reformulate the point made above, herein lies a human being's relative superiority to, and transcendence of, animality. "Every creature has to resolve indeterminacies, however trivial these may be in some cases" (FH; 163).

The classical theistic idea that God has predetermined, or at least known from eternity, all that will happen has led to the classic problem of evil: some cosmic decision must be responsible for all our troubles if the supposition is allowed that action could be wholly determined or known in advance. Hartshorne, however, as a "qualified determinist," hence also a qualified indeterminist, can:

> regard evils not as divinely imposed, or the product of some mere blind chance or necessity, but as the intelligible, though not in detail predictable, mixture of chance and necessity involved in creative freedom as universal to reality.

If every act is partly indeterminate in advance, then no power, not even divine, can have designed the world in its details, good or bad, and there is no "problem of evil" in the classic sense. (FH; 164)

The classic problem of evil implies the contradiction that there are two levels of creativity, divine and human, yet all is ultimately determined on the divine level; hence, the other level (that is, human freedom) is not really there at all. For Hartshorne, the greatest conceivable being would *want* to allow others to be free, creative; and human beings are not the only nondivine beings that exhibit such creativity (CS, 11). Human freedom causes much of the suffering that animals experience, but not all of it, as there are also diseases, accidents, natural predators, and old age. "Why suppose that only people make decisions?" People are much more conscious of the decisions they make, but if chimpanzees have no freedom at all, how much freedom has an infant? (OO; 13) Again, the argument from marginal cases is implied here.

Animals, while they cannot think about God, do feel God, according to Hartshorne (CS; 156). "How could this be?", it might be asked. Hartshorne's response goes something like this (CS; 92-95; CA; 112): If x is influenced by y, x prehends y; God influences all, hence all prehend God, however vaguely.

Some people are struck by a partial aspect of a subject and can see no other; they are logically unbalanced. "The ideal of reasonableness is to *combine balance with definiteness* (emphasis in original)." A synoptic view of things without definiteness yields "vague totality." Definiteness without a synoptic view leads to "sharp one-sidedness." Animals have the former: every animal avoids both of the one-sided extremes, both absolute determinism and the view that nothing in the future can be predicted. Higher animals at least *act* as if they take for granted that the future is partly settled and forseeable, and partly in the process of being decided. A pet dog knows that it will eat, hence it does not need to viciously prowl around to find food; yet it nonetheless whimpers when hungry out of ignorance of exactly when it will be fed. Animals so act because there is no other way they know to act. "The belief in a wholly determinate future is not translateable into action, and neither is belief in a wholly indeterminate one." Animals view the future in light of the past, without ever simply deducing it from the past. This ignorant, yet confident, feeling that animals have for the future can be none other than a feeling for God's care, dignified when found in more intelligent humanity be being called "faith." (OO; 14)

Only human beings work themselves into one-sidedness; only they are optimists or pessimists. Only thinking animals can have a monopolar prejudice.

That is, a human being's metaphysical mistakes are due to his rationality. Although ducks come to wooden decoys, they cannot be lured into a metaphysical trap, such as "all becoming is an illusion." Animals seem safe from such "perversities." So does God seem safe. It is only in the human middle ground that metaphysical error can occur.[3] Above and below human beings there can only be metaphysical truth: God's superhuman consciousness *must* know metaphysical truths (without our indistinct, fallible, and indirect knowing) (EA; 41), and an animal's action and feeling unconsciously expresses it:

> Langauge is our means of transcending the merely pragmatic or emotional sanity of the other animals and achieving a status between it and the fully conscious divine sanity. The price of this ascent is metaphysical blundering. (CS; 95)

Animals in their own way therefore may be closer to "sublime wisdom" than we humans sometimes are. They play their parts well in relation to God; human beings often live in a scheme of their own imagining. (OO; 91) Our species is the supreme image of God on this planet largely because we have elaborate reflective thinking. Yet (1) only human beings deliberately torture— God and animals do not; and (2) whales, dolphins, and primates are closer to us in reflective thinking than we used to think—in Hartshorne's comparison, they are like small children that never grow up (GN; 60).

The aesthetic version of one-sidedness is monotony, which even the birds avoid in their songs. If the basic idea of beauty is integrated diversity and intensity of experience, then bird songs are certainly beautiful. There are highly repetitive singers, but also more highly developed singers which maximize unexpectedness, although always within limits (CS; 306-307). The great majority of birds conform to the "anti-monotony principle."

The ethical version of one-sidedness is found among human beings in the contemporary dogma that self-interest is *the* principle of action for rational individuals. Strangely enough, the case for self-interest is sometimes made on the evidence of our animality: the Hobbesian war of all against all in the jungle of life is due to the beast within, we have heard. Yet as various ethologists[4] and Hartshorne have noticed:

> Not even sub-rational animals in fact derive all their other-regarding behavior from self-concern; rather they directly (though naively) seek, now to protect or help themselves, now to protect or help offspring, mates, or fellow group members. The notion that self-preservation is the law of nature is poor biology. (CS; xix-xx)

It took great genius to be as fantastically partial as some classical theists, Kant and St. Thomas among them (RS; 50; PS; 143). Kant says that God takes satisfaction in animals only because they serve the needs of God's darling, humanity. We are good intrinsically, but animals only instrumentally. This doctrine that God looks upon animals as an engineer might look upon parts of an intricate and useful machine is not one that we can take seriously in our own time. Hartshorne asks: "Why think of God at all if he is but a more extreme version of our own limitation, our own preoccupation with our sort of animal?" (RS; 50) Perhaps there is no reason whatsoever to think of such a "God."

Hartshorne's version of human transcendence of animality obviously differs from Kant's. Kant implies:

> that only a rational will that acts according to its rationality is intrinsically or unqualifiedly good. But he [Kant] also admits that human beings so act only imperfectly or incompletely and that only God always and entirely conforms to rational requirements in his actions. Consequently, only God is unqualifiedly and intrinsically good. (RS; 50)[5]

If intrinsic value rests exclusively with God (or, as Hartshorne would add, to the degree that a creature contributes to God, who is the *Summum Bonum*), then not even human beings are ends in themselves. While rational animals make a special contribution to the divine life, all creatures, especially those animals that can feel pleasure and pain intensely, make some humble difference to God. Further, Hartshorne makes a rather obvious objection to the Kantian fetish for rationality as the criterion that gives human beings absolute, or near absolute, superiority over animals: not only are adult human beings imperfectly rational, human infants are not rational at all (RS; 51; FH; 170). (Again, traces of the argument from marginal cases.) With Albert Schweitzer, Hartshorne holds that all creatures are for the glory of God, who is the only real end in itself (ER; 70). Kant should have realized this on his own premises.

Nonetheless, if there are truly general principles to the unvierse, it is the thinking animal alone who has the chance to know them. For example, C. S. Peirce believed that the higher forms of other animal life exhibited self-control and language, albeit not the great number of grades of self-control that human beings exhibit. Animals think, but they apparently do not reflexively think about thought.[6] Hartshorne feels that Plato was well advised in the *Timaeus* to employ the analogy of the "ideal animal" when trying to conceive the created cosmos as a whole (RS; 51-52). We know ourselves by being ourselves, by direct feeling or memory of what it is to be a human animal; we also know ourselves by observing other beings. We find in ourselves the positive characteristics of animals generally in the highest degree: adaptability, originality, ability to learn and remember, consciousness, and reasoning power. If we ask an atom or a plant or an ape whether there is such a think as creativity or reason, we will not receive an answer. But we human beings, although we can answer this question, are intelligent enough to realize the

> difference between zero and a finite positive quantity makes *all* the difference when we are seeking the general principles of reality. (RS; 52)

It should now be clear that the development of a theory of human commonality with animals is not necessarily at odds with the thesis that human beings transcend animals in some important ways. The question I will ask in the next chapter is: To what extent can such transcendence justify the treatment of animals as resources for our use?

It should also be clear that there is no incompatibility between suggesting that animals deserve our respect and suggesting that suffering caused to us by innocent subhuman creatures "puts pressures on us to act in our own interest and for our own need, even regardless of the needs of others" (CS; 238). One way to support this latter suggestion is to note that human beings can worship God, whereas animals cannot do so. (NT; 4-6). Although animals can feel God, as discussed above, they cannot worship, if worship refers, as Hartshorne thinks, to consciously and explicitly being aware of oneself as an individual who is nonetheless a fragment of the whole of things. A sentient creature feels and acts as one in that its sensations and desires are its own sensations and desires. But it does not consciously and explicitly engage in such an act of integration. That is, the ideal worship depends on rationality; hence those who live without worship are more like the nonhuman animals than those who live with it. Because we are animals, nontheism is always an option open to us. Or more precisely, if someone were to claim that there could be a nontheistic worship of The Unknown or of Nature as a Mystery, then animals, too, have worship. The major difference between an agnostic and an animal, for Hartshorne, is that the latter has integrity as an individual within a larger whole, whereas the former tries to place his individuality within a grander, integrated whole but does not quite know how to do so. Luckily for both the theist and the agnostic, there is animal innocence to fall back on.

A fetus crosses the line from subhuman to human, hence at one stage in its development the fetus shares an animal's innocence. (Although before the development of a central nervous system the fetus is, in a sense, in a pre-animal condition, as St. Augustine implied.[7]) Therefore, if killing a fetus in the later stages of pregnancy is bad, killing a whale is far worse on the evidence of its superior brain, sentiency, and behavior, and on the evidence of the argument from marginal cases. (OO; 100-103 and WM; 49, 119) This consideration of animal innocence has provided a convenient bridge to Chapter Five and ethical issues concerning animals.

Chapter Five

Foundations for a Humane Ethics

Viewing all objects unremittingly
In disconnexion dead and spiritless
And still dividing, and dividing still,
Break down all grandeur . . . waging thus
An impious warfare with the very life
Of our own souls . . . .
This beast not unobserved by Nature fell,
His death was mourned by sympathy divine.

Philosophical vegetarianism and other expressions of ethical concern for animals flourished in ancient Greece,[1] then died out in the West, for the most part, for fifteen hundred years or so, largely because of Judaism and Christianity as traditionally conceived. Recently, however, the phoenix of concern for animals has arisen once again.

In the contemporary philosophical debate over the status of animals, two arguments, in which our duties to animals are considered, stand out above the others. These arguments, from sentiency and from marginal cases, were stated briefly in Chapter One. It will be remembered that the argument from sentiency asserts the right of any being that can feel pain (S2), or which values its life, not to have pain or death inflicted on it unnecessarily. And the argument from marginal cases holds that there is no characteristic which all human beings posssess (including the marginal cases of humanity) which is not also possessed by the higher animals, hence if the marginal cases of humanity deserve respect, then so do animals.

For Hartshorne, it should be noted that if God, the "supreme parent," cares for all sentient beings, even for the fall of a sparrow (OO; 46; CA; 135), then to be cruel to animals is to contribute to vicarious divine suffering (OO; 28).[2] No human being can fully share in the experiences he helps others to enjoy or suffer. "The final harvest from every seed sown is reaped by God."

This is God's cognitive and perceptive perfection. The cross is Christianity's sublime symbol for the vicarious suffering or unselfishness of God. (OO; 120–121) We can certainly suffer in a greater number of ways, and in more complex ways, than animals. But this does not give us a carte blanche to inflict suffering on animals in whatever way we wish. (OO; 128) Theological statements regarding a human being's supposedly extremely privileged status cannot be philosophically justified, nor is it even clear that they can be consistently supported on biblical evidence, depending on how seriously one takes the law of *agape*.

Before indicating Hartshorne's support for these two arguments, let me briefly return to his theory of freedom, which provides the background against which his adherence to these arguments is to be understood. "The reality of genuinely open notions implies a fundamental aspect of tragedy in life" (FH; 164). That is, a partially indeterminate world means that no laws of nature or divine providence:

> can guarantee perfect harmony among individuals, human or nonhuman. Set the banks of the rivers as close as you like, but there must still be some free play among the particles . . . . Life itself requires that there be some room for the self-determination of each moment of life in each individual career. And if this self-determination is limited to trivialities, then life itself becomes trivial. (FH; 165)

The source of all vital harmony is the same as the source of all disharmony, freedom.

> All any ruler, or any providence, can do is set wise limits to the options; but so long as there are options at all, and life at all, there will be possibilities of discord as well as of concord. (FH; 165)

Human freedom is dangerous because it threatens not only human beings but all life on earth. Contrast here Western humanity, aided by advanced technology, with the American Indians. They were aware of their responsibility to existing life, but their methods could support only a small human population, and even this small population in a way that limited human potential. These quantitative and qualitative restrictions were used by the white settlers as excuses for appropriating Indian land. Whatever quantitative and qualitative progress Westerners were able to squeeze from the land, however considerable, was no boon to animals, and ultimately may be no boon to human beings, either. There was a recent furor when twenty-three American eagles were found illegally and needlessly killed. Why such an uproar over these animals when thousands of animals are needlessly (albeit legally) slaughtered every day? Only because the eagles symbolize our own freedom? Or because they are an endangered species? And why should this bother us? Because *our* enjoyment of nature will diminish if they become extinct? What about concern for *each* animal that suffers or is killed unnecessarily?

Hartshorne finds it a curious defect in most Western ethics that self-interest is absolutized. He contrasts the ethical view to mere self-interest; the former he approves, not because it is good for you or me, but good for at least some class of individuals from an interpersonal, long-run point of view (FH; 166). The attempt (à la Adam Smith) to deduce altruism from intelligent self-concern is only a disguised self-interest. If one enjoys sympathetic feelings for others only because it secures one's own happiness, then one is (perhaps unwittingly) using sympathy as a ruse for an "ethics" of self-interest:

> The self, identity, or indivduality that is thus taken as the absolute end is nothing absolute at all, but in many ways is highly relative. Each moment I am a new reality identical only abstractly, or partially and in outline, with what existed before. In deep sleep I am not, as a conscious being, actual at all. And in death what will I be? (FH; 166)

Animals have a more balanced attitude than egoists:

> They absolutize neither their own individuality nor that of their fellows, but relate their momentary needs to some of the needs, not altogether momentary, of others. (FH; 166)

Along comes reason, as some conceive it, and self-interest becomes "enlightened." But it may well be that the absolutizing of self-interest as an end in itself is itself an *un*enlightened superstition. What reason generalizes above the merely personal in ethics is not mere self-concern nor just altruism, but "the whole complex of self-regarding and other-regarding impulses."

In the long run we will not be here; only the everlasting whole of things will be (FH; 167). Perhaps this fact, if nothing else, should humble us into a consideration of animals:

> One difference between ethical principles relating us to our human fellows and those relating us to the rest of the animal kingdom is that both sides to an interhuman dispute can appeal to principles *qua* principles, while the nonhuman side to an infrahuman dispute cannot do this. How close to such a thing chimpanzees can come remains an interesting question. (FH; 167)

By this test, however, even a human infant or a mentally enfeebled human being would fail. Enter the argument from marginal cases.

The point to the argument is not to deny respect for infants or the like, but to positively attribute something to animals. If human beings without reason have actual rights, then:

> I say that horses and apes have them in a stronger sense. Their nervous systems, and hence their experiences, are functioning on a much higher level. (FH; 167)

Humans are ethical beings because they use symbols. They do in a conscious, generalized fashion what animals and infants and the mentally enfeebled do in an unconscious, particular way: They all contribute to the cosmic drama. It is true that human beings are the only creatures that, in addition to vividly empathizing with other creatures , which some animals can also do, can clearly and definitely put before themselves the question: "whose values ought to give way in the case of conflict?" (FH; 168). Only human beings can see themselves as trustees for a cosmic, divine end, or "an all-inclusive value vaguely understood." It is just this value, in the distant as well as in the near future, with which religion at its best is concerned. Science is essentially concerned with this value, too, but specialization within this endeavor has blinded most of its practitioners to this fact.

All will agree that the parts of an animal (its cells) have their value primarily, if not entirely, in their contribution to the whole animal. "But when the inclusive or cosmic whole is considered, we hesitate" (FH; 168). Politics misleads us here, for a good state is one that merely fosters and protects its parts, that is, individuals; "There is no further good actualized in the state as an individual entity." And biological groups such as families and cultural groups such as the American Philosophical Association have successive generations that inherit roles and purposes, but not their very being. Metaphysical societies, however, do have such an inheritance. Cultural societies are like trees, some with diseased cells ruining the others. A cultural society would be monarchical in the metaphysical sense if there were something like a Teilhardian "group mind," but only if this were the case. As it is, despite vast differences among human beings all of them are equal when contrasted to cells, and most of them are equal when contrasted to most animals (leaving room for the argument from marginal cases). Thus the poltical problem for humans is to organize activities in the absence of a metaphysical monarchy. (IS; 73-81)

The cosmos is different, where an organic analogy is more appropriate than a political one, as Plato realized when he compared the created cosmos to an animal. Unless we use such an organic analogy, the dictum that God is to be loved with one's entire being either makes no sense or appears totalitarian. If we feel kindly toward animals then:

> the religious meaning of this must be that they, too, are valuable to God, so that in loving them we are loving something in God himself. To the extent that we fail to love life in its myriad forms, to that extent is our being outside our love for God. Have Christians, Jews, or Moslems done justice to this simple reflection? (FH; 169).

A few, at least, have; this was noted in Chapter One. But even these (for example, St. Francis) were in need of the sort of rational reflection and categories Hartshorne gives. Unfortunately, Hartshorne must share the indignation of a thinker like Schopenhauer at the indifference of traditional Christian beliefs to the sufferings of animals (IO; 192–193).

Hartshorne asks the following, rather startling, question:

> Though human beings have (let us grant) a net superiority to the other animals, may it not be the case that there is a price for this superiority, so that in some significant respects we are actually inferior. (FH; 169)

In what ways are human beings inferior? We have previously seen that only they are metaphysical blunderers, but more important, only human beings are conscious trustees for a cosmic end. In that animals are unconscious workers, they are:

> infallible servants of the cosmic cause. By inherited arrangements they are guided in the right paths. (FH; 169)

What evidence does Hartshorne have for this claim, which must seem incredible to the speciesist? Animals care for themselves and their young; they try to help their mates and fellows within their species; in some cases animals cooperate across species lines.[3]

Animals are as "altruistic as a competent naturalist would want them to be." Apart from dietary considerations, lions eat meat because they know of no other way to eat. Gunton should have realized this when he expressed the desire for God to act as a lion over an antelope (see Chapter Two). Human symbolic power, however, extends the scope of altruism and other-regarding behavior. The price of these powers:

is the capacity to reject the duty (to serve the cosmic cause) as well as to perform it. We can refuse our implied trusteeship. The other animals cannot. They do their best. Man may or may not do his best. So man is the grandest and the sorriest animal there is. (FH; 170)

As has been argued previously, in the sense in which any animal has intrinsic value, all animals have some of it, and as the argument from sentiency indicates, animals that can experience pleasure and pain intensely as wholes or as individuals have a greater degree of it than others. It perhaps seems reasonable to assign human beings (even nonrational ones) a far higher value than even sentient animals, but even this does not deny value to animals, especially the higher animals. If ethical concern were a pie of a fixed size, then giving a slice to animals would deny something to a deserving human being. But ethical concern and *agape* are seemingly boundless things, and even if they were not, by refusing to eat animals or kill them for clothing, etc., we are not really doing anything to them or giving them something a human being could use more profitably. Rather, we are *not* doing something to them, *not* giving them the bludgeon or the knife of the abattoir. (RS; 59) Human value, as many "primitive" people realized, is additional to or complementary to the values of others, rather than competitive with them (FH; 170).

This is difficult for modern (speciesist) people to understand or accept. Or is it? Do not most people implicitly accept the argument from sentiency? That is, do not most people see a significant *analogy* between a dog in pain and a human being in pain? And that, other things being equal, we should prevent or at least mitigate the dog's pain when it occurs or threatens? (FH; 171) There are laws, as is well known, about not causing unnecessary pain to pets. If only there were more laws (or laws) and more ethical concern dealing with cows, pigs, endangered species, et al. It is true that death does not destroy the reality an animal has already achieved, in that God cannot forget an animal's experiences once they have become actual; this is part of God's perfection, (OO; 33-36) But does this admission deny the claim that we should prevent or at least mitigate the dog's pain when it occurs or threatens? (FH; 171).

And analogize with humanity we must. Weak-minded analogies in the Bible (God as jealous, etc.) based on human experience are no worse than falling into the opposite error of making God (or animals) totally unlike the only reality we live through, the human. What does it mean to say that human beings are in the image of God if God is immutable? And how can an unmoved God love? "A well-meaning attempt to purify theology of anthropomorphism purified it of any genuine, consistent meaning at all" (OO; 28-30). As

Ralph Waldo Emerson put it, all turtle thoughts are turtle, but the turtles do not know that. We have the idea of "idea." Hartshorne anthropomorphizes only to the extent that his thoughts are human thoughts, albeit purified of many of the inconsistencies of previous attempts to think about the relationship between subhuman and superhuman reality.

As human beings, we are more valuable than other species, but we do not know if we are infinitely more valuable. We are mortal in the same sense as other creatures, save for the difference that we alone can consciously contribute to the beauty of the whole of things, a beauty which survives us (FH; 171):

> If we avoid absolutizing man's difference from the rest of nature, we can more easily open our minds and hearts to the really infinite difference, that between any mere animal or mere transitory creature and the Primordial and Everlasting. (FH; 171-172)

Judges and the police are supposed to defend legal rights; "moral" rights, as Hartshorne uses the term, are acknowledged by the conscience of the community at large; and "ethical" rights are those that sufficiently enlightened, or reflective, or disinterested, or knowledgeable individuals would support (RS; 49). Regarding animals, few are enlightened, or reflective, or disinterested, or knowledgeable enough to attribute ethical rights to them. There are some otherwise intelligent and ethical people who would even find the very topic of the present book, quite apart from the arguments therein, frivolous or trivial or useless. Thus, before animals have their moral rights acknowledged by the (meat-eating) community, they have to receive them from (meat-eating) philosophers and theologians.

How likely is this? I do not know; but there are certainly more philosophical vegetarians in the West now than at any time since antiquity. And three great Eastern religions (Jainism, Buddhism, and Hinduism) teach, at least for their sages, the duty of respecting life, especially in its animal forms, and derive the ethical superiority of a vegetarian diet from this duty (RS; 49). The justification for these positions sometimes relies on transmigration, because to kill an animal may be to kill a past or future human being. But as was the case among ancient Greek vegetarians,[4] vegetarianism has been defended in the Orient on grounds other than transmigration. If our Western religious faith is in a God who takes delight in creation, unlike some Oriental views, should we not *especially* take animals and their rights seriously?

> Whatever importance we, and those we can help or harm, have is without residue measured by and consists in the delight God takes in our existence. Is it likely that God takes no delight whatever in the more than a million other living forms on this planet, yet does delight in, derive value from contemplating, the one human species, lately emergent on the planet? If such an idea is not sheer anthropomorphic bias, what would be such bias? (RS; 50)

No doubt the deity is vastly less inhibited in sympathies than human beings. Love fundamentally, for Hartshorne, consists in "life sharing" or "delighting in the lives of others" (RS; 51). This is true on the human and divine levels. Our love is different from God's in the limitations of the scope and quality of our sharing; only God sympathizes with and takes delight in "all the forms of life" (RS; 51). Hartshorne nonetheless believes that our love can and should extend beyond our own species (WM; 35).

An apparent snag appears in Hartshorne's thought here. If God loves all forms of life, and if we are to imitate God to the extent that we can, how do we account for the fact that no creature can live without treating at least some other creatures as less important than itself? (We should remember from Chapter Three that, for Whitehead, life demands food, which requires robbery, which calls for justification.) A response to this question must rely on the realization that importance is a matter of degree:

> A logical requirement of any value system is that it should clarify the idea of no value, or the value of zero. I hold that, as value diminishes, its limit of zero is to be sought not in a form of existence without value, but in total nonexistence. The zero of feeling, or of instrinsic value, and of actuality are one and the same. (RS; 54)

On this account even plants have value, but not so much value that we can fear hurting them. The argument from sentience should force us to realize that there are gradations in the animal world, such that the case to respect animals weakens as one goes "down" the evolutionary scale from mammals or birds, to fish, to other sea creatures.

Let me quote Peter Singer once again on this point to provide a friendly amendment to what I think should be Hartshorne's views on animals given his distinction between S1 and S2:

> Those who want to be absolutely certain that they are not causing suffering will not eat mollusks either; but somewhere between a shrimp and an oyster seems as good a place to draw the line as any, and better than most.[5]

This is a prudential line being drawn; but drawing it between a cow and a chicken or fish would not be a prudential judgment at all, as it would in effect ignore S2 altogether.

Hartshorne's own way of aesthetically classifying forms of life is rather novel (RS; 54-55). Creatures which exhibit a unified variety are "pretty" if they have a low degree of intensity and complexity; at the other extreme, "sublime" creatures exhibit greater intensity and complexity; the "beautiful" lies somewhere in between. Where variety is insufficiently unified, the "ridiculous" or the "funny" occurs if intensity and complexity are not great; and the "tragic" if intensity and complexity are very great. Because the categories Hartshorne uses apply across species lines to include human beings, animals, and perhaps even plants, which can be "pretty," there is nothing unique to human beings about having the above properties. Many animals are beautiful, some (for example, koala bears?) are pretty or cute, others (for example, grizzly bears?) are sublime. Unfortunately, funny animals are often exploited in circuses and zoos (but not always in zoos); and perhaps most important, animals that are slaughtered or have their natural habitat stripped from them can be tragic. Even sparrows can *fall,* as Jesus noticed.

For Hartshorne, ethics is subservient to aesthetics. Either ethical principles are special aspects of the aesthetic ones above or they specify the means that indirectly favor aesthetic categories (RS; 55). Not only do spectators sense beauty in observing a genuinely good person, but the good person becomes good by sympathizing with the *feelings* of others. It is no accident that the Greek *aisthesis,* from which we get "aesthetic," meant "perception." It follows that those who are not good, or not as good as they seem, make the world "uglier, less harmonious, or more tedious, less zestful and intense" (RS; 55). The fact that our culture pays little attention to the intimate connection between ethics and aesthetics is a defect. The human species has more appreciably developed the moral dimension of value than the animals, but not necessarily to the complete exclusion of the aesthetic dimension. Both birds and human beings make music, but the former do not reduce the aesthetic dimension sufficiently to allow the moral dimension to grow.

Another approach to the idea that ethics is subservient to aesthetics goes as follows: in order to find out what we are as individuals we must in some way show an interest in others. These others include our bodily cells, which we *feel* directly, if not distinctly (CA; 135), as well as other human beings, animals, and plants. Altruism explains self-love, not the other way around (OO, 108; CA; 3). If love is the concern of "life for life, experience for experience, feeling for feeling, consciousness for consciousness, freedom for freedom," then a religion of love can encourage us to "look upon nature as a realm of love and freedom," whose members are images of God (OO; 111-112). We may finally come to appreciate the ancient principle that love is the principle of principles (OO; 61). "Intrinsic value gives power" in that I can only feel because my cells feel; my sense of goodness must intuitively take the goodness of cells into account. "Hurt my cells and you hurt me. Give my cells a healthy life, and they give me a feeling of vitality" (OO; 80-81). Nonetheless, to love others as we love ourselves is an absolute ideal that we often fall short of, but not God (OO; 123).

Relying on John Cobb, Hartshorne touches on another snag in our relations with animals.[6] We value each human being individually, but "we tend to think that one nightingale or one hermit thrush is significant chiefly as a specimen of its species" (RS; 56). Perhaps this is because individual differences are rather slight in birds, perhaps also because birds do not have a concept of self-identity; but as the argument from marginal cases indicates, neither do many human beings whom we respect as individuals. Although the death of a bird is vey different from the death of a human being, we must keep in mind that Birdhood or Cowness never suffer, but *this* bird or *that* cow do. No doubt our giving individual names to pets largely accounts for the preferential treatment they often get in comparison to other animals. But even rats have become pets. (EA; 178) And Hartshorne himself admits that when a rabbit mates or escapes the fox it has its own individual purposes in doing so (MN; 92).

Animals cannot be murdered, but the unnecessary killing of animals by human beings is close enough to murder that a case can be made against hunting for sport or the wanton slaughter of animals (RS; 56). By regulating the population sizes of animal species, we legitimately subordinate other species, but this is a far cry from the uncalled-for extermination of individual animals, and more drastically, whole animal species. Once again, aesthetic considerations interpenetrate with ethical ones:

> To a nature lover it takes a lot of conveniences to balance a radical diminution of natural beauty. Suppose the more than seven hundred species of birds in this country were reduced to one hundred, and in any one state from two or three hundred to two or three dozen, would life remain as interesting? Not for some of us. The lovely prairie grass is gone. Every lawn begins to look about like every other. How much monotony do we want? Only a few species of trees flourish in our cities. Our parks lack the rich undergrowth that many species of animals require, and so they are dull places, scarcely better than the tiny backyards of the urban poor. (RS; 57)

If it were necessary to kill a single bird to save a human life in some hypothetical situation, then perhaps the bird should be killed. Each of us is of more value than many sparrows. (WM; 27; ER; 71-72; RS; 51, 57; FH; 171; OO;46) But how *many* more? This is a difficult question, especially as regards the use (often abuse) of animals in medical experimentation. While so many in our culture still enjoy their fetish with cigarettes, millions of animals are killed on the modern altars of Asclepius to find a cure for cancer. Are these deaths necessary? Hartshorne himself hypothetically suggests that he "could perhaps seriously consider giving up the remainder of my life it it would definitely save a threatened species for millenia" (RS; 57). That is, it is an open question as to whether any one of us is of more value than a whole sparrow species (ER; 72). Some solace is received by knowing that however animal and human values are distributed, they all add up to a significant whole in the divine life (IO; 115, 216).

Moving away from hypothetical weighing of interests, Hartshorne concretely proposes that the burden of proof when wild nature is destroyed or, I might add, when animals are needlessly killed, is not with the preservationist or the vegetarian (RS; 57). Even on anthropocentric grounds the burden of proof is often on those who kill animals. When it is considered that cows are, when seen as food-producing machines, like Cadillacs, then on purely human grounds vegetarianism may be in order. (IO; 224) Because it takes between ten and twenty pounds of grain to get one pound of beef, these wasted pounds of grain are, in effect, denied to starving human beings, of which there are millions. Very little of the enormous yield of crops in the American Midwest is directly eaten by human beings, only indirectly through the inefficient cows and pigs used as food machines.[7] Complete vegetarianism, for Hartshorne, may not be the most appropriate solution to this problem of feeding the world's starving humans, but its potential contribution should be noticed. As a civilized people we no longer need to serve meals like pioneers (WM; 34).

The artificially high limits set by human beings to the reproduction of edible animals is therefore an offense to the "inclusive ecosystem":

> But the fact, now dawning upon all, that our greedy exploitation can boomerang upon ourselves or our children may in time lead our species to save some substantial portions of the wonderful tapestry of life on the surface of this globe. Yet the change of attitude must come rather rapidly if this is to occur. For the destruction of the nonhuman goes on rapidly indeed. (RS; 58)

Once again, this should bother us even on anthropocentric grounds:

> We are the only animals capable of being interested in, finding some use for, taking some delight in, *all* the forms of life. This is why zoos and botanical gardens exist. But wild nature has values that such artificial vessels can never more than partially contain. Even from the selfish human point of view this is true. Thus one finds some of the famous species of songbirds in zoos, but so crowded together that what one hears from them is a discordant, confused, frustrating blend of noises, nothing remotely like the symphony of distinguishable voices one may hear at daybreak in a forest or wild savannah. (RS; 59)

Quite ironically, in the very century in which we have made most progress in understanding the lives of other animals, we have killed, or threaten to kill, not dozens or hundreds but thousands of animal species.[8]

The following rough ordering of values would seem appropriate from Hartshorne's aesthetic point of view, at least in our present state of culture where so much of nature has been destroyed or is threatened with destruction:

> allowing animals to live in the wilderness
> wildlife management
> keeping domesticated animals as pets
> killing animals unnecessarily in laboratories or for the table.[9]

Obviously this does not mean that domesticated animals should be ignored though they are not tortured. The point is that our fetish for pets often works to the disadvantage of animal species taken as a whole. One is reminded here of Peter Singer's delightful story of an acquaintance who declared herself an "animal lover" while offering him a ham sandwich.

Indifference to the instrinsic values of animals often leads to losses in the instrumental values these animals have for human beings. Selfishness toward others not surprisingly leads to an injustice toward our own selfish interest. The problem is largely an educational one (RS; 59). Ignorant city dwellers, commercially minded farmers, and indifferent suburban residents are not primitive, but their uncultured attitudes toward animals make them a new kind of barbarian (RS; 60). There are limits beyond which our technological empire over the animals is either intolerable or self-defeating (ER; 71).

As rational animals, we should also consider the extent to which our own procreation affects animals. It is undeniable that each additional person adds value to the world; it is also the case that each additional person detracts value from the world, at least if he or she lives off animal flesh, or carelessly takes or ruins the air, food, or water upon which animal life depends. Hartshorne tries to avoid one-sidedness here (ER; 71-72). Exclusive concern with animal species, as opposed to individual animals, is callous. Yet an animal killed in a slaughterhouse or by a hunter nonetheless could (perhaps not on factory farms) have enjoyed the brief life it had. What is more bothersome to Hartshorne, it seems, is if individual animals and, even worse, animal species are slaughtered or extinguished. Then not only is a particular animal treated unfairly, but its species-dependent mode of enjoyment itself comes to an end. (ER; 72)

The Book of *Job* demonstrates a feeling that animals have their own values which, at the very least, should force us to reconsider our desire for luxuries at the expense of animals (ER; 72-73). We must be critical of advertisers and friends who tell us (explicitly or implicitly) that the good life means a life of many possessions, which directs us, perhaps unwittingly, to be cruel to animals (ER; 73), as in cosmetics being produced only after being tested on cats, who are blinded in the process. It is a Christian commonplace, yet also a largely untested hypothesis, that spiritual possessions are more important than material ones. If animals and the environment in general are to be spared, some people at least must give up some things. "How hardly," in Hartshorne's helpful translation, "shall a rich man enter into the kingdom!" We have done poorly by this text, he thinks (ER; 74), to the point where even our notion of a "square meal" needs rethinking (ER; 76). Wild nature on this planet may be doomed, and a great deal of domesticated nature as well, unless Christians and Buddhists and others live like saints. When so many abuse animals, or fail to meet their duties to animals in other ways, supererogation is needed from others.

The counter-culture of the 1960s and 1970s was, in a way, correct: it is a new day, yet one in which the Greek and Oriental sages of old must be thought about again. "To be a functioning human being in a functioning universe is already and in itself a glorious thing" (ER; 77). The element of chaos in the midst of this glorious reality, however, is not due, as one of the authors of *Job* thought, to divine will, but is a tissue in the heart of reality itself:

> What is this chaos? Quite simply, it is multiple freedom, self-determination of the many impinging upon the self-determination of each one. As Plato said, more truly than he quite knew, the soul is self-moved, and the secret of all motion. No god and no human arrangements could guarantee perfect order or harmony, either in human life or in the world anywhere. (ER; 77-78)

Just by choosing to plow the ground we may accidentally kill snakes. With good luck the multiple decisions of human beings may fit together harmoniously; bad luck is more likely (ER; 78). It is "mere superstition" to suppose that "ideal" or divine power could conceivably eliminate all risks which inhere in concrete actuality. Yet luck or no luck, much of animal tragedy can be avoided by more considerate choices made by the freest, yet most dangerous, animals—human beings.

Before leaving ethical issues, it might be profitable to narrow the gap between my explicit defense of vegetarianism and Hartshorne's (and John Cobb's) overtures in favor of vegetarianism without their making any definite statement in favor of the position.[10] I will narrow this gap largely on the evidence of Hartshorne's and Cobb's own positions.

Cobb, the great student of Hartshorne, agrees with Hartshorne that there is a new level of experience in animals not found in plants. Hence, both would agree, I think, that it is only permissible to eat animals if they are treated in a fair way while alive, and are slaughtered in such a way as to be rendered unconscious "instantaneously," so that they are killed "without pain." (This ignores for practical purposes Hartshorne's theoretical claim that although given perceptions for animals—including human beings—are "present" epistemically, they are not, for all we can tell, simultaneous temporally with their causes—CA; 179).

Although this leaves meat eating open as a theoretical option, there may be a practical imperative to become a vegetarian in contemporary society because of the unlikelihood of these conditions being met. The deplorable conditions on modern factory farms have been ably documented.[11] Here, animals are merely increments of capital. To take one sort of animal as an example, chickens do not gambol about in a farmyard; they are raised in cages barely bigger than their own bodies, in need of debeaking so as not to peck each other to death out of frustration; and incredibly enough, they are in need of contact lenses (yes!) so as not to perceive their neighbors, nor be chagrined by the fact that they live their entire lives in the dark.[12] If, by chance, a door in a huge henhouse is opened and a shaft of light breaks through, pandaemonium breaks loose.

But if animals were treated fairly and killed without pain, what case could be made for killing them for food? Cobb cites three points: (1) The death of one chicken may make room for the raising of another, such that the loss of value has been replaced. Cobb is to be criticized here on two grounds. First, Cobb's utilitarian reasoning whereby one quantity of value can be sacrificed if another replaces it, is precisely the sort of reasoning that Cobb himself (as well as Hartshorne) has spent a great deal of time criticizing. Second, even if Cobb's version of the "replaceability argument" shows some concern for animals, it is really only the (supposedly) Platonic form of "Chickeness" which is reverenced, not the particular chicken killed, which is the real locus of value in Hartshorne's and Cobb's own views.

(2) It does not seem that the quality of a chicken's life is pervasively affected by the anticipation of its death. Three responses are in order, the first of which is an obvious use of the argument from marginal cases. Many human beings (the comatose, et al., as well as those in their youth) do not have the quality of their lives pervasively affected by the anticipation of death. Second, even if chickens do not anticipate their death, their pleasure at seeing sunlight after long periods of deprivation of light makes it difficult to claim that they do not value their lives. They certainly act as if they do. And third, even if chickens do not anticipate their death, cows do. Farmers have numerous stories about how cattle and pigs willingly get onto a truck unless it is the time for the final ride, when they resist. Especially belligerent on the truck, they resist even more at the slaughterhouse when they smell the blood of their fellows. In vain they try to turn around in their narrow chutes. Whether this anticipation of death on their part pervades their lives I do not know, but it is not clear if this is a relevant consideration anyhow.

(3) The death of an animal poses no significant hardship to others in the way the death of a human being affects family and friends. Three remarks here: First, the aforementioned effect on cattle of the death of their kind should not be totally ignored. Second, we should realize that veal calves, when permanently taken from their mothers, cause nothing short of grief in the mothers for quite some time afterwards. Other mammals in family groups (for example, baboons) show even more despondency when one of their own dies. Third, pigs, who have in some rural areas been adopted as pets by human beings, often score higher on intelligence tests than dogs. And it does seem premature, to say the least, to claim that dogs experience no significant hardship when one of their kin (or their "master") dies.

Cobb does admit that chimpanzees show signs of individuality and the other criteria that would perhaps prevent us from killing them, but, because there are so few of them and because we would probably not like their taste as food, this is a small concession. More significant is Cobb's disapproval of the slaughter of porpoises by fishermen trying to catch edible fish. Is there a nonarbitrary way of commisserating with chimps and porpoises but not with pigs, cows, chickens, and fish? I think not, but the formidable plant–animal distinction regarding S2 is acknowledged by Hartshorne and Cobb *themselves*.

Hartshorne clearly shows support for that variety of vegetarianism based on a concern for efficiency of protein resources, but this is ultimately due to a (legitimate) concern for human welfare. Hartshorne's wonder is whether a few moments of suffering near the ends of their lives cancel out the hundreds of thousands of moments when animals do not suffer. Using the Lucretian insight, he also notices that dead animals do not suffer. Once again, there may be a practical imperative in favor of vegetarianism if an animal-commodity has more than just a few moments of suffering spread throughout its whole life.

Hartshorne is on stronger grounds, I think, in his implied use of immortality theory. The social immortality of the Old Testament, where only some of the experiences from the past are remembered, is inferior to the objective immortality of Whitehead and Hartshorne, where all creaturely experiences are immortalized in the divine life, which cherishes all that happens to creatures. This is what allows Hartshorne to suggest that the vast majority of pleasant experiences an animal has cannot be cancelled out at the end of its life. But then neither are the painful experiences nor the anticipations of death—however dim—nor the unrealized potential for pleasure terminated in each healthy animal killed. The sadness is that all of *these* "contributions" to the divine life are completely unnecessary in that human beings can live quite healthy lives off plants. This ought to be the key to vegetarianism from the perspective of process theism.

It should now be obvious that I have emphasized individual animals as individual, but without a substance-oriented doctrine of the self or a Leibnizian theory of identity. Rather, my position rests of the claim that unnecessary moments of pain and premature and ugly modes of dying ought to avoided.

None of what I have said is meant to deny Hartshorne's major insights regarding animals. Rather, I think that my "immanent critique" makes vegetarianism the logical outcome of Hartshorne's own position. As we have seen, Hartshorne more than once uses a version of the argument from marginal cases. Does the argument not override one of Hartshorne's other legitimate claims, that many human beings make plans for the future, and every moment of our lives gets part of its meaning from this, whereas animals do not make such plans? Yet, not all human beings make such plans for the future.

I can also agree with Hartshorne that mortality as such is not an evil, and that it is premature or ugly modes of dying, rather than dying *simpliciter,* that are evils. I have only tried to point out how unnecessary, hence premature and ugly, are the deaths of animals specifically raised for the table. It must be granted that terms like "premature" and "ugly" must be used analogically when applied to animal deaths, but they must be used nonetheless. Even though animals largely concentrate on the here and now, and although their expression is largely emotional or practical, without an abstract, reflective grasp of their place in the scheme of things, they as well as human beings contribute to the undying, inclusive life of the everlasting being in becoming, God.

Hartshorne is also correct in noting that the greatest evil we do to animals is to destroy their habitat, for then we take everything from them; to kill a whole species is worse than killing individual animals, because to kill a whole species is to kill massive numbers of individual animals, perhaps threaten the existence of other species, and diminish the world from an aesthetic point of view. But this does not deny that we can do other great evils to individual animals even if we preserve the animals' species.

We should also notice that Hartshorne's doctrine of relations has ramifications for the issue of vegetarianism. An example of an external-internal relation is grass being eaten by a cow or a vegetable being eaten by a human being (remembering, however, that the microscopic parts of grass and other plants do have internal relations). But this relation changes greatly when a cow is eaten by a human being. (CA; 140) A cow that is treated as a food machine while alive, that senses its own immanent death at the slaughterhouse, and that experiences pain in the transport to the slaughterhouse, and intense pain moments before its death, is capable of internal relations; hence eating it seems to be an internal-internal relation.

As before, Cobb's Hartshornian definition of ethics, as the heightening of importance given to internal relations, is instructive here. For as long as we are willing to kill and eat animals when it is not necessary to do so, and as long as we treat domesticated animals as increments of capital on modern factory farms, it is difficult to see how we will show any more concern for animals in the wild unless it is in our own anthropocentric interest to do so.

Suffering looms larger in humans than in other animals largely because sickly humans are less likely to die, humans do not have predators other than other humans, and humans make long-run plans that often fail. Hence, in general, animals are not sick and happiness is primary. Further, they live largely because they *want* to do so. For these reasons there is no need for sentimentalism when we consider the fact of animal death as such. A further reason not to mourn animal death as such is that young animals find life new and exciting; old ones find it less intense and tepid. However, although it makes little or no difference to an animal (other things being equal) whether its death is brought about by a predator, by lightning, or slaughter by a human being, it does make sense for *us* to notice that the infliction of unnecessary suffering or death on an animal is wrong. That is, we can distinguish among: (1) a human murder of another human; (2) a human killing an animal unnecessarily; and (3) an animal killing another animal. (1) is far worse than (2), which, in turn, is far worse than (3), which is morally neutral. (WM; 53, 55-56, 58, 60)

Chapter Six

Contributionism and Wordsworth

If something from our hands have power
To live, and act, and serve the future hour;
And if, as toward the silent tomb we go,
Through love, through hope, and faith's transcendent dower,
We feel that we are greater than we know . . .
Ye blessed creatures, I have heard the call
Ye to each other make; I see
The heavens laugh with you in your jubilee
My heart is at your festival,
My head hath its coronal.

In the previous chapter I stated that one reason to be opposed to the unnecessary infliction of suffering or death on animals is that the pain animals experience and their premature, ugly deaths affect God. In the present chapter I will emphasize how important this reason is. Further, I will deal with an important predecessor to Hartshorne, Wordsworth, who provides an important link along the Plato-romanticism-Hartshorne chain that I am emphasizing in this book. Not least among the features in Wordsworth we should notice in his belief that the contributions we make to the divine life "will ever be."

Because it takes time for ethical (or moral) decisions to have their effect, all ethical obligations in principle concern the future. Hartshorne links this fact with an organic (not political) model of the universe, which enables him to conclude that "the entire rational significance of the present is in its contribution to future good" (EC; 103). This does not mean that present happiness is of no value. Rather, Hartshorne's view is a positive one regarding the present, unlike some other views of the present. Its value is not cancelled out by its becoming past. This preservation of value is effected partly by our remembering past happiness, but more importantly by being "inherited by the cosmic or divine reality that cherishes all creatures."

The rational aim of life, when human transitoriness and divine everlastingness are considered, is to contribute value to the future, including the value of present happiness. Only a totalitarian, political view of the universe would see this claim as sinister. On the organic view of the universe we can easily say with St. Paul (and Peirce and Buddha): "We are members one of another." Ultimate obligations are to God, not to any person or persons or animals. Yet notice the two ways in which we can fulfill our ultimate obligations: "By achieving our own happiness and furthering future happiness in other persons *or animals* " (emphasis added) (EC; 104). In fact, even animals themselves can make contributions to other animals, for example, to their offspring (EA; 188). The more remote the future in question is, the greater the danger that we will make mistakes in our calculations. Some actions are obviously to be denigrated, say energy waste or land abuse, on anthropocentric grounds. A grave defect in our culture is that we seldom take seriously other contributions we could make to the future. Saintliness, among other things, means making modest demands on the labor of others, the suffering of animals, and the depletion of other natural resources. Something worse than "mere bad taste" is involved in our profligate attitudes toward animals.

Hartshorne sees no incompatibility in defending the individual rights of persons and animals and claiming that our ultimate obligations are "to the future in an impersonal or superpersonal sense, to humanity, to nature, to God" (EC; 105). Individual rights in ethics do not necessarily have to be based on a rigid metaphysical theory of individual substances:

> The whole idea that our final obligation is to groups of animals, whether human alone or (as I would say) human and subhuman, is to my mind utterly inadequate. Here all religions largely agree. If the cosmos has no value, neither, by any rational standard, do animals or persons. The parts are for the whole, the ephemeral for the abiding. And the only aspects of the whole that we can influence or benefit are future aspects. I call this doctrine *contributionism.* It is essentially Whitehead's view, and I regard it as implicit in all the religions. (EC; 106)

Unfortunately, religious tradition is shot through with human, all too human, error. Yet we should love ourselves especially because we are valuable to God (OO; 107). Just as people have done poorly by the second commandment of Jesus—to love the neighbor as the self—so have they done poorly by the first—to love God will all one's being (OO; 121). To follow the first commandment would nonetheless force us, for practical reasons at least, to have special responsibilities for our own welfare, in that there are many benefits that no one can give to us unless we give them to ourselves (OO; 124).

Animals live largely, although not exclusively, by feeling; we live, we have to live, far more by thought (EC; 107). Feeling applies to all concrete singulars; consciousness or knowledge, only to higher levels of reality, including animals. Or better, there are physical aspects of feeling, which give one a sense of the past, and mental aspects of feeling, which give one a sense of the future and the ability to think. So whatever is conscious and can think can also feel, but not vice versa, unless "consciousness" is taken in the broadest way. (EA; 38-39, 128)

Yet in recent centuries human thought has been largely devoted to technological pursuits. Hartshorne is quite openly a romantic, at least in the sense that he believes that what technology produces is not necessarily a better life for those not on the brink of starvation (ER; 69). Aristotle, Shakespeare, and Thoreau lived lives on a high level. Technology essentially does two things well: (1) it incredibly increases the numbers of those for whom the best is available; and (2) it allows a great number of people at least a marginal existence. These points make us realize that Hartshorne, although a romantic, is not a naive one. Cobb catches Hartshorne's sense when he talks of our "fall upward," whereby each advance in civilization brings with it dangers. Whitehead said in "Peace" at the end of *Adventures of Ideas* that there are always the (romantic) dream of youth and the harvest of tragedy. Technology not only makes kingly luxuries available to large numbers, it even makes luxuries beyond the reach of the kings of old, for example, automobiles, which Hartshorne has not owned, because "these luxuries are not essential to life on a high level" (ER; 69; IO; 225). Not even printing is necessary for that (although literacy may be). The American Indians, who perhaps only numbered several million after thousands of years in North America, knew:

> loyalty, democratic self-government, love of spouse and children, sense for
> the beauties of nature, reverence for the divine, humor, zestful rivalry, poetry,
> music (ER; 69-70).

Western culture was able not only to expand this list, but also to expand the number of people who could enjoy these things. There is at least one group, however, whose lives have not been enlarged by technology—nonhuman living creatures. As humanity has expanded, most of the other animals have decreased. The humpbacked whale, with its well-developed song and an intelligence that rivals the apes', is threatened with extinction; rats, however, thriving on our waste, are more numerous than ever (ER; 70). In many parts of North America, deer are more numerous than ever, but this is because we have destroyed the habitat for other wild animals: wildcats, beaver, wolves, and others.

Two examples of four-term analogies can illustrate Hartshorne's cosmology and contributionism. The first (inadequate) analogy compares the world as a whole to an inert table, even if there is human significance in the world:

microscopic sentiency (S1) : table ::
sentient animals, including human beings (S2) :
non-sentient world.

The process theist, however, sees the world differently. Consider:

microscopic sentiency (S1) : sentient animals,
including human beings (S2) :: sentient animals,
including human beings (S2) : World Soul or God (S3).

Imagine the following thought experiment (EA; 184): if we looked at a telescopic motion picture of some large segment of the universe taken over a period of millions of years but played back within one hour, might we not see some familiar, purposive, organismic actions? Also, imagine an opposite experiment slowing down immensely microscopic action. Do not S1 and S3 become more understandable through these experiments, even if only performed in imagination?

"God is everywhere," the catechisms taught us, but did they explain as well as Hartshorne how this could be so? The ubiquity of deity forces us to take Plato's God, the World Soul or the ideal animal of the *Timaeus,* quite seriously (IO; 251). That is, for Hartshorne religion not only helps us to better understand animals, but analogously *deity itself* is a sort of superanimal (IO; 342)! God, or the World Soul, is the "individual integrity" of the world, the society of individuals in the world brought together as a single individual (OO; 59). As in Chapter Two, this God can be seen in a dipolar way, not entirely unlike each of ourselves, viewed as constantly changing yet preserving the same abstract identity through change. "God's field of distinct perception is the de facto whole itself," which paradoxically makes God in a way more like the other animals than like us: for animals' perception is instinctively of their "whole" environment, rather than concentrating on certain aspects. God's perception is of the real whole. Human beings pay a price for their microscopic analyticity (OO; 93-94). With full clarity, God, if God is greater than any other being, preserves all value; our entire worth is imperishable in the divine life. As St. Paul asks, "O Death, where is thy sting?"

One of the most powerful similar visions of nature—opposed to the technological imperative to do all that can be done with our means of construction and destruction—was offered by Wordsworth, whom Hartshorne (like Whitehead[1]) admires. T. B. Macauley was wrong in describing Wordsworth's thought as "crazy metaphysics" (DW; 80). Surprisingly, Hartshorne thinks that science, which Wordsworth largely detested ("We murder to dissect"), has vindicated the master's position. Eighteenth- and nineteenth-century science was essentially materialistic in its view of inanimate nature, and dualistic in its view of human nature. And philosophy in England then "offered no persuasive alternative to these views." Classical physics was noted for its mechanical view of nature, in which the world was seen as a machine made up of pieces of inert matter moving through space according to deterministic laws. By "inert" is meant lack of the ability to move oneself, or to actualize one's own possibilities—creativity—and to appropriate external influences for oneself—sentiency.[2] This view became enshrined in Newton's three laws of motion.

By way of contrast, recent physics has made materialism and dualism problematic, and has made Wordsworth's view of nature more plausible than ever. It is true that quantum mechanics has been variously interpreted. All will agree, however, that the view that physical processes are spatially and temporally continuous must be dropped, even if macroscopic objects do conform to the thesis of continuity. Atoms do not travel from one energy state to another in a smooth motion; they do so in discrete, quantum jumps. Atoms "jump" because they are subject to forces from other particles. The "free" particle (even in quantum mechanics) has a continuous spectrum of *possibilities* of motion, but there are no completely free particles. Every particle has an existence defined by its relations with others. "What *are* the 'things' that jump?," one might ask. Some physicists have argued that we are dealing merely with numbers or mathematical entities; others defend a pragmatic stance in which quantum formalism does not reveal the essence of the physical world, but it does work in experimental situations.

Hartshorne and Wordsworth are obviously more interested in metaphysics, broadly conceived in Wordsworth's case, but this does not mean that their views are necessarily at odds with the pragmatic interpretation of quantum mechanics. Both are very much interested in how we experience nature, or, speaking crudely, what works for us when we try to explain the world. The principle of indeterminacy made famous by Werner Heisenberg led some (for example, Einstein) to speculate that hidden variables would be found to save absolute determinism—these hidden variables have never been brought to light. At the very least, this much must be said about the effort to speculate metaphysically on the basis of discoveries in contemporary physics, which even some physicists have been driven to do: we cannot understand microscopic (or submicroscopic) events on the analogy of macroscopic objects like billiard balls, yet it is precisely these latter objects which give us our notions of inertness and determinism. To know with assurance that active singulars are not sentient is to have Godlike knowledge, but why would God create such entities with no intrinsic value (MN; 91)? Hartshorne alerts us to the fact that what is not discussed in physics is not denied by physics (GN; 61).

This fact does not give us carte blanche, but it does give us freedom to take Wordworth's view of nature seriously, as does Hartshorne. Wordsworth's view includes the following features (DW; 81): throughout animate nature, even plant life, there is feeling; so-called "inanimate" nature is not really inanimate; nature as a whole expresses a unified Mind-like reality, of which lesser lives are participants; in our perceptions of nature we at least indirectly experience these features; but most civilized people are not aware of these truths, because after childhood they lose the experience of nature, being preoccupied with supposedly more practical concerns; these ignorant or forgetful people claim to know that most of the universe is "dead matter," whatever that means.

In "Lines Written in Early Spring," Wordsworth talks of birds:

Their thoughts I cannot measure:—
But the least motion which they made,
It seemed a thrill of pleasure.

And plants:

The budding twigs spread out their fan,
To catch the breezy air;
And I must think, do all I can,
That there was pleasure there.[3]

Wordsworth is in danger at this point of losing all ability to discriminate among parts of nature if both birds and twigs are sentient.

Hartshorne contends that Wordsworth was not committed to any implausible view here (DW; 82). He did not necessarily imply that the entire tree is a sentient individual; he is only committed to the view that in its small—perhaps invisible or microscopic—parts the tree's "twigs" (not the whole tree) are sentient. Nor was Wordsworth a naive realist who directly intuited the feelings of birds or plants. Our most direct contact with physical reality is with what happens inside our bodies, especially in our nervous systems; only then do *we* perceive reality *through* our cells and nervous systems. If human sensation is participation by persons in the feelings of subhuman individuals (that is, cells), then it makes sense to suspect that the same is true for other animals who have nervous systems similar to ours.

In physical pain or pleasure we share in the feelings of microindividuals. Following Whitehead, Hartshorne calls sympathy "feeling *of* feeling." Feeling itself, if not feeling of feeling, "goes far down in the scale of organisms" (DW; 83), far below birds or fish. So far below, that, as noted in previous chapters:

> mere dead, insentient matter is a pure construct, not a datum. We do not know what it would be like to experience such a thing. Should not our thoughts about nature be in harmony with what nature is as experienced? And *as* experienced, nature consists of feelings . . . . Whitehead's description of nature as "an ocean of feelings" sums up the conclusion. (DW; 83) (emphasis in original)

Psychicalism for Hartshorne is unfalsifiable in so strong a sense that it practically implies "true" (EA; 40). Nothing could be easier than to accuse Wordsworth of the pathetic fallacy. Consider these lines from "The Simplon Pass," also found in *The Prelude* (Book VI):

> Brook and road
> Were fellow-travellers in this gloomy Pass,
> And with them did we journey several hours
> At a slow step. The immeasurable heights
> Of woods decaying never to be decayed,
> The stationary blasts of waterfalls,
> And in the narrow rent, at every turn
> Winds thwarting winds, bewildered and forlorn,
> The torrents shooting from the clear blue sky
> The rocks that muttered close upon our ears,
> Black drizzling crags that spake by the wayside
> As if a voice were in them, the sick sight
> And giddy prospect of the raving stream,
> The unfettered clouds and region of the heavens,
> Tumult and peace, the darkness and the light—
> Were all like workings of one mind, the features
> Of the same face, blossoms upon one tree:
> Characters of the great Apocalypse,
> The types of symbols of Eternity,
> Of first, and last, and midst, and without end.

But the pathetic fallacy is committed here only if one is a materialist or dualist, the latter view prohibiting animate characteristics being read into inanimate matter, the former view prohibiting animate characteristics being read into nature at all. The question is not whether winds were really bewildered or forlorn; rather Wordsworth asks us about our experience of winds, which appear to us as feelings. And, as contemporary physics at least allows, the winds themselves in their microscopic parts may feel. "Physical things come into our experience only as feelings" (DW; 84). Might not Wordsworth's opponents be committing a more prevalent fallacy: the apathetic or prosaic fallacy, which is to assume that all reality, or most of it, is like an insentient chair? Of course there are reasons for believing rocks and chairs to be inanimate: they are motionless, they lack freedom, individuality, and intrinsic purpose. But how strong is the evidence that all of reality—atoms as well as God—is rocklike? Not too strong. It seems to be Hartshorne's and Wordsworth's opponents who are open to the charge of illegitimate anthropomorphism by exaggerating the role of human qualities at the expense of other animals, supposedly inanimate nature, and God (MN; 91, 94-95).

Hartshorne's defense of Wordsworth against the charge of committing the pathetic fallacy goes as follows:

> The cells of a plant fit the requirement (sentiency) better than the entire plant, and even more obviously do molecules, atoms, or particles fit it than do winds, rocks, or rivers, tables or chairs. And we know quite well what it is in animals, but not plants or rocks, that enables the entire animal to act and hence feel as one. This is the nervous system. Yet single cells act as one, and naturally without a nervous system since that consists of many cells of a specialized kind. A nervous system has the function of restoring of a higher level the unity of action (and feeling?) which single cells, as well as single molecules, have on lower levels. (DW; 85).

The view of nature held by Wordsworth, primitive animists, children, and at least some who are familiar with contemporary science, may win out yet. Life and feeling, in many forms, pervade and constitute nature; this is what Hartshorne calls "psychical monism." "The cosmic machine of the 18th century has become the 'cosmic dance' of the 20th" (DW; 86). Although contemporary science does not exactly prove Wordsworth right, it cannot prove him wrong.

Each of the three views has a price: (1) Dualism admits feelings or experiences to persons, at least, but it strikes many as an admission of defeat in the attempt to explain animate creatures, that is, dualism leaves the psyche unintelligible or insufficiently related to body. (2) Mere materialism or behaviorism not only fails to explain mind, but it also leaves matter as an empty abstraction. And (3), psychicalism's price is that it makes us aware of our human or animal incapacity to share in feelings radically different from those produced for us by our own nervous systems.

But this price is easier to pay because of Wordsworth, whose:

> glory is that he gave matchless poetic expression to one of the three options for thought, an option to which disciplined inquiry now imposes fewer obstacles than it did 180 years ago. (DW; 86).

The vaguely theistic implications of Wordsworth's last line quoted from "The Simplon Pass" link psychicalism or panpsychism or psychical monism with theism, or better, with Hartshornian panentheism. In feeling ourselves to be fragments of reality we indirectly feel the whole of which we are fragments; this is the metaphysical side to contributionism in ethics (DW; 87). Because we only have own own experience as a model for the All-Inclusive, nothing like divine immutability is suggested in the poem—in fact, the opposite is suggested by Wordsworth's use of "eternity." Wordsworth's religious view of nature sees it as the receptacle for the happiness of its creatures:[4]

> It is not, so far as I can see, in the spirit of Wordsworth to regard the happiness of creatures as simply superfluous additions to a supreme reality or deity defined as entirely self-sufficient or independent, eternally complete in itself (the classical definition, illogically combined with the doctrine that God loves the creatures). The creatures are not wholly external to their creator. . . . At times Wordsworth seems to fall into the opposite or pantheistic trap, according to which God is merely the cosmic totality of individuals, not a self-active super-individual. But this is not a necessary interpretation of his poetry. (DW; 87).

Hartshorne parts with Wordsworth's belief in personal immortality, or at least with Wordsworth's intimations of it. Yet the two are not totally divided on this issue. Wordsworth shows faint agreement with Hartshorne's and Whitehead's belief in objective immortality, one form of which is related to contributionism:

> A kind of immortality . . . is already implied by the view that our lives are somehow embraced within the divine life. We can be included in a living and everlasting whole without being endless in our duration; yet our finite careers, all our experiences from birth to death, can never cease to be constituents of the Inclusive Life. For, if we human animals can retain in memory, though

faintly and partially only, the careers of our deceased friends, the Inclusive Life can do so in uniquely excellent fashion. There are some of us who have no wish for more immortality than that. (DW; 87-88).

If there is such a thing as mere lifeless, insentient matter or process, then most of the world is devoid of intrinsic value and is therefore amenable to human manipulation. This is why feelings in nature are no trifling matter. If nature is a mere means to our ends, it can be exploited, and the romantic's case is ruined, at least if the God in question is one who cares for the whole of creation. Paul Weiss puts the issue this way:

> Instead of taking ultimate units to be just filled-in regions of space, each substantial, persistent, and inert, Whitehead and Hartshorne hold instead that they have privacies and in effect are "living" units, coming into being and passing away, moment after moment, but not without preserving and transmitting what had already been achieved. (EA; 117).

This seems to have been Wordsworth's view as well.

Hartshorne commends Wordsworth for giving up determinism. If freedom is identified, as British philosophers have often done, with voluntariness, then the religious significance of freedom is missed. (DW; 89) The question is not: Do we do what we want to do uncoerced by fear, passion, etc.? Rather, the key issue is: Are we, in part, creators of the world, "further determiners of a partly indeterminate reality? The dignity of the individual is in the power to settle, here and now, what all the past, and divine power, have left unsettled." (DW; 89)

Divine creativity does not settle the details of cosmic history. It is only human beings, when imitating God as tyrant, that try to do this. Creative freedom even in animals means a pervasive element of real chance in the world. Thus, some conflict and frustration are to be expected. But when Wordsworth's universal psychicalism is forgotten, and all of nature is enslaved, or a dualism of free and unfree portions of nature is imposed, making the unfree parts amenable for enslavement, then and only then is conflict and frustration in nature made the rule rather than the exception.

The following Hartshornian diagram may help illustrate his and Wordsworth's cosmology in terms of the distinction between mind *(m)* and body *(b)*, with capital letters referring to God and small letters referring to creatures:

$$(1)\ Mb \qquad (4)\ Bb \qquad (7)\ MBb$$
$$(2)\ Mm \qquad (5)\ Bm \qquad (8)\ MBm$$
$$(3)\ Mmb \qquad (6)\ Bmb \qquad (9)\ MBmb$$

This diagram is an exhaustive list of the various theistic options available for the mind-body relationship, the first column listing the options regarding God as pure mind; the middle column regarding God as pure body; and the last column regarding God not as a being divided into two reified substances, but as a single yet dipolar being.

Options 1, 5, 7, and 8 do not seem to be represented by any great figure from the history of philosophy. Option 2 was Berkeley's view; option 3 that of Aristotle and the classical theists in Judaism, Christianity, and Islam, with minor differences in each; option 4 was that of Hobbes. Hartshorne humorously cites option 6 as the possible view (although this is unlikely) of Philo when he suggested the world was a great vegetable.

Hartshorne's own dipolar view of God and creatures is option 9, with M and *m* referring to the organic, novel responses to the past of which all concrete singulars are capable. B and *b* refer to the causal inheritances which concrete singulars receive from the past, making rather routine or reiterated responses prevalent, say, in an "inorganic" rock, but less prevalent in human beings. Hartshorne avoids dualism by claiming that soul or mind includes body, and not vice versa.[5] As before, terms like "being" and "body" are abstractions which refer to aspects of units of becoming; body is an aggregate of sentient units of process. If what I prehend most intimately is my mind-body, and if God prehends in a supreme way on the analogy of human prehending, then it makes sense to talk about the world (specifically all of the feelings in the world) as constituting God's body.

Some might object that to make all creaturely life a means to the divine life is to make God selfish. But is it selfish to want a healthy rather than a sickly body (GN; 60)? And is not the greater danger regarding divine selfishness to be found when we altogether abandon Plato's mind-body analogy for the cosmos, and make God, like Kant does, a cosmic policeman?

The mistake that most interpreters of Wordsworth make is to assume that divine immanence and transcendence are mutually exclusive. One of my theses in this chapter is that Wordsworth was neither a pantheist nor a classical theist. Throughout his career, his works bear the stamp of panentheism. As late as 1835, when many see him having completely abandoned his supposed earlier pantheism, he states: "And nature God disdained not." Wordsworth's theism was always a nature-oriented theism of some sort, and at odds with classical theism. Yet at least as early as 1804, when some suggest he did not see God as transcendent, we can see him talk of God as:

> the Upholder of the tranquil soul,
> That tolerates the indignities of Time,

And, from the centre of Eternity
All finite motions overruling, lives
In glory immutable.[6]

A pantheistic God does not uphold souls, nor can it be described in such Platonic terms. But we shall further discuss Plato in the next chapter.

More fruitful that a genetic approach to Wordsworth's theism is my hypothesis regarding his lifelone panentheism, which, when used as a heuristic device, is quite fruitful. Has justice been done to these famous lines?

And I have felt
A presence that disturbs me with the joy
Of elevated thoughts; a sense sublime
Of something far more deeply interfused,
Whose dwelling is the light of setting suns,
And the round ocean and the living air,
And the blue sky, and in the mind of man:
A motion and a spirit, that impels
All thinking things, all objects of all thought,
And rolls through all things.[7]

Granted, the presence that disturbs Wordsworth rolls through all things, dwells in setting suns, the oceans, the air, and in the mind of man. But this presence also *impels* all thinking things, implying that this presence has some sort of independent existence on its own.

More accurate than the suggestion that God is in all things is the claim that all things are in God, meaning that all that happens in the world makes a difference to God. The mind of man becomes:

In beauty exalted, as it is itself
Of quality and fabric more divine.[8]

God cares for us even when the world, which is different from God's being, if not from God's becoming, does not. Wordsworth speaks:

In gratitude to God, Who feeds our hearts
For His own service; knoweth, loveth us,
When we are unregarded by the world.[9]

If these lines are inconsistent with pantheism, those in the remarkable selection below are equally inconsistent with classical theism. Do they not indicate that Wordsworth's theism was a panentheism, which, again, means "all *in* God"?:

> All beings live with God, themselves
> Are God Existing *in* the mighty whole.[10]

It is premature to hold that "If any language is pantheistic, this surely is."[11] If these lines mean that the whole is greater than the sum of the parts, which is a tenable interpretation supported by many other texts, then Wordsworth's language here is not pantheistic. As St. Paul says (2 Corinthians 12): "The body is one and has many members, but all the members, many though they are, are one body, and so it is with Christ."

Trying to have one's cake and eat it too is impossible; crying like Plato's child for both being and becoming, for divine transcendence and immanence, is not impossible at all:

> Listen! The mighty Being is awake,
> And doth with his eternal motion make
> A sound like thunder—everlastingly.[12]

God is not only "mighty Being" but also "eternal motion." In fact, it is largely God's eternal motion, unlike our temporary or intermittent motion, which makes God such a mighty Being. Regarding the sounds of a mountain echo, Wordsworth tells us to:

> Listen, ponder, hold them dear;
> For of God—of God they are.[13]

But concerning a seashell he says, at the same period in his career, that:

> Even such a shell the universe itself
> Is to the ear of Faith; and there are times
> I doubt not, when to you it doth impart
> Authentic tidings of *invisible* things.[14]

Divine perfection lies, he implies, in dipolarity. After viewing Leonardo's "Last Supper," Wordsworth notices: "The *love* deep-seated in the Savior's face."[15] Yet Wordsworth also believes that the superiority of the Christian God to pagan deities (nature deities!) lies in God's *impenetrability*.[16] Wordsworth avoids the conflict found in classical theism when it claims that God is both an unmoved mover and a God of love. That is, for Wordsworth God is impenetrable because God's love is *so* deep-seated.

What have previous interpreters of Wordsworth's concept of God done with the following lines treated above, written about rocks and clouds? They:

> Were all like workings of one mind, the features
> Of the same face, blossoms upon one tree:
> Characters of the great Apocalypse,
> The types and symbols of Eternity,
> Of first, and last, and midst, and without end.[17]

God is not only one, which even the pantheist could admit, but one *mind*. It is not only the defects in pantheism that Wordsworth corrects, but also those, perhaps primarily those, of classical theism: "The immortal Mind *craves* objects that endure."[18] It is true that Wordsworth calls God "Eternal Lord!"[19] And he holds that:

> The wise man, I affirm, can find no rest
> In that which perishes.[20]

But he also believes, and not inconsistently, that God breathes,[21] and has a love which remains unquenched.[22]

All can agree with Wordsworth that the term "God" refers to "Supremacy,"[23] But what does it mean to be supreme? To exist necessarily and to be steadfast, yes; but also to be merciful,[24] or better, to be a fountain of grace,[25] a God of peace.[26] Supremacy consists in a harmonious balance of flexibility and duty, which is the "stern daughter" of God's *voice*.[27] Notice below, on the one hand, the words "sorrow" and "friend," and on the other, "never":

> Oh! There is never sorrow of heart
> That shall lack a timely end,
> If but to God we turn, and ask
> Of Him to be our friend![28]

Wordsworth's panentheism is evident not only in the poems treated above, which were written in the wide period between 1798 and 1837, but also in his masterpiece, *Ode: Intimations of Immortality*. Wordsworth wishes his days to be bound with "natural piety," and considers youth as "nature's priest," but is in fact this theism, which has come to terms with nature and has linked nature with God, a pantheism? What is little noticed is that the blessed events in nature which participate in the divine life are "Creatures," with whom heaven laughs. The term "creature" makes no sense without a Creator. Nor is it often emphasized, although it is mentioned, that Wordsworth's theism is an affair of the mind as well as the heart: his "*head* hath its coronal." We are in the life of God in that God knows us, feels us, loves us. But Wordsworth believes in a God "who is our home," and we are not *fully* at home in this our own world. The child is the one who is a "mighty prophet, seer blest," with "heaven-born freedom." We adults notice that the visionary gleam, the glory and the dream, of our home has faded. However:

> We will grieve not, rather find
> Strength in what remains behind.

My claim is that panentheism is one of the things that remains behind, for us perhaps an acquisition of the "years that bring the philosophic mind." We human beings are dipolar, but not supremely so; we become, and yet have an identity through time. God's supreme becoming speaks to us through the rainbow that comes and goes; through the birds, as Hartshorne more than anyone knows; and through timely utterances. Concomitantly:

> Our noisy years seem moments in the *being*
> Of the *eternal* silence.

It might be objected that my panentheistic interpretation of Wordsworth is highly unlikely, because he never read Hartshorne, nor did he ever consider Whitehead's distinction between God as primordial and God as consequent. This charge may be a bit too hasty, however. Although the word was not used in antiquity, panentheism, or at least dipolar theism, is as old as Plato. It has been noticed that one can be a Platonist without knowing it.[29] The same can be said about being a panentheist. At least with regard to Platonism, Wordsworth was a self-conscious participant, as is Hartshorne, as we will see in the next chapter. He said to Emerson in 1848 that if the *Republic* were published as a new book, it would have few readers, yet "we have embodied it all."[30] "We" refers at least to Wordsworth himself and S. T. Coleridge, but perhaps also to the Cambridge Platonists, Thomas Taylor (with his researches and translations), and Schleiermacher (especially his *Introduction to the Dialogues of Plato*), all of which were well represented in Wordsworth's library at Rydal Mount.[31] Wordsworth refers to "Plato's genius," his "lure sublime," and the "everlasting praise" due to him. His truth is that "half of truth" most neglected in

England.[32] The other half, widely accepted, was the Aristotelian tradition of empiricism. One scholar goes so far as to claim that the revival of interest in Plato may be the most important single facet of the Romantic movement.[33] In short, if Plato were a panentheist, it would not be an exotic guess to suspect that it was through him that Wordsworth got his panentheism. And Hartshorne explicitly tells us at several points about his debts to Wordsworth and to Plato's theism. He says: "I have always been something of a Platonist" (EA; 165).

Certain Platonic texts are obvious sources. In the *Sophist* (246–249), the Eleatic Stranger develops the mature Platonic metaphysics, which is opposed by both the "giants," who are the materialists (or, we might say, the pantheists) who drag everything down from the heavens to earth; and the "gods" (or, we might say, the classical theists), who defend their position somewhere on the heights of the unseen. Reality is dyadic for Plato, and is constituted by anything (being or becoming) which has *dynamis,*the power to affect or be affected by something else. Even in the *Republic* Plato avoids what many readers of Plato have assumed to be the Platonic position: unbridled worship of being. The task of the philosopher (501B) is to glance frequently in two directions: first, at the forms of justice, beauty, and the like as they are in the nature of things, but also at this cavelike world, where one must try to reproduce the forms to the extent that one can, or at least recognize the extent to which material justice or beauty participate in formal reality. As has often been noticed, but seldom understood fully, Wordsworth had a yearning for the One underlying the many, but also an appreciation of the extent to which each of the many was itself possessed of a certain degree of unity, or else each of these would not be *a* tree, *this* deer, etc.[34]

Perhaps the most convincing studies of Plato's theism and the dyadic character of being in Plato have been done by Leonard Eslick. He relies on Hartshorne, whom he cites as the first to recognize Plato as a dipolar theist.[35] There are two significant ways in which Plato talks about God *(theos)*. First, Plato inherited from Parmenides the notion that being is eternal, immutable, and self-same. It is this notion that was the starting point for the tradition of classical monopolar theism. "The extent to which Plato is committed to such an absolute schism between *being* and *becoming* . . . would seem to dictate for him a similar exclusion from divinity of all shadow of change."[36] This tendency is evidenced in Book Two of the *Republic,* the *Phaedo* (78–80), and the *Symposium* (202–203). However, as Eslick and others hold, there is no textual foundation for the popular identification of Plato's God with the transcendent form of the good, nor even with the world of forms, either as a whole or in part.[37] Even when talking about divine eternity and immutability, the Platonic locus for divinity is *psyche* or *nous*. It comes as a shock to some readers of Plato who have only read the *Republic, Phaedo,* and *Symposium* that in the *Phaedrus* (245, etc.) Eros is claimed to be divine. Here Plato discovers, according to Eslick, a new, dynamic meaning for perfection, similar to the one described above, and exemplified in the selections I have chosen from Wordsworth.[38] The perfection that is dynamic is the perfection of life itself, treated not only in the *Phaedrus* but in Book Ten of the *Laws* as well.

In the *Timaeus* and the *Sophist,* both poles in Plato's theism are brought together: the perfection of divine immutability and the perfection of divine life. The former is identified in the *Timaeus* with the Demiurge, who eternally and without change contemplates the archetypal models, the eternal forms. Divine life is identified with the World Soul, which is close to Wordsworth's and Hartshorne's panpsychism, and whose essence is self-motion, and who is depicted as posterior to the Demiurge.[39] The motions of psychic life include both actions and passions. In fact, in the *Sophist,* as has been noted above, and as is the case in quantum mechanics, reality is identified with *dynamis* or power; specifically, the power to affect or be affected by others. (It is no accident that it is from this word that we get our word "dynamic.") Even Aristotle attests to the fact that reality, for Plato, is the *joint* product of the One and the Indefinite Dyad.[40] Unfortunately, Aristotle's own notion of God loses the Platonic character of divine immanence, of God as the Wordsworthian or Hartshorian soul of the world. Even more unfortunate is the fact that Plotinus, and others who became identified as followers of Plato, were with respect to their descriptions of God really Aristotelians.

It is not unreasonable to speculate that Wordsworth saw the inadequacies of latter-day Platonists. We have seen that he claimed about Platonism that "we have embodied it all." In the following poem Wordsworth indicates that truths about God can be searched for in terms of a Platonic piety. God is the immortal one, hence solitary; but also a builder, although Wordsworth was always sceptical about talk of God as a creator, even if he himself engaged in such talk at times. God is above the starry sphere, hence dark, yet not alone in that God whispers to us and allows us to see God.

> Yet Truth is keenly sought for, and the wind
> Charged with rich words poured out in thought's defense;
> Whether the Church inspire that eloquence,
> Or a Platonic piety confined
> To the sole temple of the inward mind;
> And One there is who builds immortal lays,
> Though doomed to tread in solitary ways,

Darkness before and danger's voice behind;
Yet not alone, nor helpless to repel
Sad thoughts; for from above the starry sphere
Come secrets, whispered nightly to his ear;
And the pure spirit of celestial light
Shines through his soul—'that he may see and tell
Of things invisible to mortal sight.'[41]

Caution must be displayed when putting Wordsworth into a category, or when affixing a label to him. But even those Wordsworth interpreters who make this point themselves categorize Wordsworth and affix labels to him, at least if they *are* interpreters. The trick is to avoid egregious errors in categorization, and to affix labels without dogmatism so that the texts themselves can breathe. To call Wordsworth a pantheist or a classical theist (or even an orthodox believer) is to leave unexplained something significant in Wordsworth's thought. To call him a panentheist is to get a little closer, I think, to his thoughts on God. Yet when dealing with thoughts as rich as those of Wordsworth, too deep for tears, getting a little closer may be going a long way.[42] In any event, it is time that the Plato-Wordsworth-Hartshorne tradition of viewing God as a superanimal receive its just due.

The ultimate goal of the treatment of Wordsworth and Plato here is threefold: (1) to show Hartshorne's philosophic roots, treated inadequately by previous scholars; (2) to show how panentheism enables us to take animal feelings seriously as elements in the divine life; and (3) to show how a consideration of an animal body helps us understand divine inclusiveness and transcendence.

The similarities between Wordsworth and Hartshorne should now be obvious, and Hartshorne's debt to Plato has been alluded to throughout the book. In the next chapter I shall make this debt explicit in a detailed analysis of Hartshorne's Platonism.

Chapter Seven

Hartshorne and Plato

For love, that comes wherever life and sense
Are given by God, in thee was most intense
A chain of heart, a feeling of the mind,
A tender sympathy, which did thee bind
Not only to us Men, but to thy Kind:
Yea, for thy fellow-brutes in thee we saw
A soul of love . . . .
Accept, mute Captives! thanks and praise;
And may this tribute prove
That gentle admirations raise
Delight resembling love.

As I made clear in the Introduction, this is a book primarily about Hartshorne's thought on God and animals. Every chapter deals with both of these topics, although some chapters deal with one more than the other. The present chapter, like Chapter Two, deals more with God than animals, but not to the exclusion of the latter. In fact, the notion of God as the ideal animal is one of the most important ideas explicated here.

As before, I have alleged that behind Hartshorne is Wordsworth, and behind both is Plato. By the end of this chapter not only will the Plato-Hartshorne axis be clearly drawn, as it concerns God and animals, but also the other figures in the history of philosophy who lie on this axis or who cross it at right angles will be appropriately mentioned. Further, an analysis of the Platonic notion of soul—including animal, human, and divine soul—is crucial for understanding Hartshorne's philosophy.[1]

Because of his famous remark that all of Western philosophy is a series of footnotes to Plato, and because of his equally famous defense of the concept of "eternal objects," Whitehead is often thought of as a Platonist. Yet, despite Hartshorne's use of Plato's thoughts on the World Soul in the *Timaeus,*

Hartshorne is hardly ever compared to Plato, because Hartshorne is some sort of critic of "eternal objects." My thesis in this chapter is that Hartshorne is every bit a Platonist as Whitehead.

Hartshorne favors the view that suggests the dialogues can be considered stages in Plato's intellectual development, looking at Plato's later dialogues as the more significant account of his position. The principles in the early dialogues are retained in the later, but they are used within a more profound system of concepts, just as Plato's thoughts can be used by neoclassical metaphysicians like Hartshorne without Plato's being affected by their speculation. (It should also be noted that Hartshorne's thoughts on the asymmetry of Plato's dialogues (PS; 38-39) are perhaps the best clues we have as to how Hartshorne would have us regard his own philosophic career, particularly the flurry of works he has published since he turned seventy.) Although it is too simple to say that there is an inverse relationship between the emphasis placed on the theory of forms and that placed on God, it does seem fair to say that there is a shift in meaning in Plato's thought when teleological explanation according to forms is modified in the later dialogues by teleological explanation in terms of God.

What does it mean to explain the world? At the very least it means to elucidate the unitary principle behind the apparent duality of mind and matter. Plato wavers, for Hartshorne, between seeing this principle in the forms and seeing it in soul *(psyche)*. Hartshorne emphasizes the difficulty in offering an explanation through forms, which is not really an explanation through soul; that is, the forms are items internal to psychical process (IO; 23-24).

If "X is independent of Y" has a sharp logical meaning it must be that X could exist even if Y did not, which implies that Y is contingent. If X stands for the forms and Y for God, then the nonexistence of God is being taken as possible. But this "possibility" conflicts not only with the treatments of God in the *Timaeus* and Book Ten of the *Laws,* but also with Plato's flirtation with the ontological argument.[2] If the Demiurge is *not* contingent, then not only are the forms envisaged by deity, they *could not* fail to be so.

If one asks whether the forms have supremacy over God, Hartshorne's response is that "the issue is secondary and largely verbal" because Plato implied the noncontingency of theism (PS; 56-57; WM; 15). The good and God are both eternal, and "independence" has no clear meaning between eternal (or everlasting) things. Only the most extreme "Platonism," not necessarily held by Plato, would see abstract entities as real in themselves apart from *all* concrete embodiment, say, in some concrete process of thinking. The basic reality is concrete, even if the most fundamental abstraction is "concreteness". Metaphysics itself is "the study of the abstraction 'concreteness'." Hartshorne is not so bold as to claim that Plato *quite* saw that concrete actualities are the whole of what is, but he came close enough to seeing this in his thoughts on God in the later dialogues so as to confound traditional interpretations of Plato's forms as absolutely independent of concrete embodiment (CS; 22, 100).

Hartshorne believes that Whitehead follows the neoplatonists and Plato himself (and, indeed, Hartshorne) in holding that forms as eternal objects are divine ideas, "nothing simply by themselves" (WV; 9). And our physical prehensions (which animals also have), and our hybrid prehensions of God as having these ideas, are our best clues as to how to acquire them for ourselves. The disagreement between Hartshorne and Whitehead has nothing to do with the latter's relying on Plato and the former's eschewing Platonic influence. Rather, the major point of difference seems to lie with the question as to which ideas are eternal in God and which are acquired (divinely or humanly or in an animal-like ways) as the creative process goes on.

Hartshorne thinks that Plato hints at the psychicalist position when Plato indicates that soul is coincident with every action and passion. But no Greek was in a position to fully understand the difference between singulars and aggregates in the smaller parts of nature. Although Plato could not fully understand the cosmological significance of panpsychism, it would be a mistake to think that he was totally ignorant of its significance, either by returning to primitive animism (all things are full of gods) or by defending dualism *simpliciter.*

The meaning usually assigned to Plato's theory of forms was really born in the first book of Aristotle's *Metaphysics*, according to Hartshorne. Hence the greatest problem in Plato's cosmology is not this theory of forms, but that of sufficiently grasping the functions of soul as both creative and receptive, and the related problems of understanding internal and external relations and how soul interacts with body. (IO; 27-28; CA; 208-209)

It is an error to assume that Plato's alternative to being determined by the past is to be determined by an ideal, for no ideal can be applied without creative particularization (IO; 34). Hartshorne's theory of creativity can readily be seen as "the Platonic one" when "create" is substituted for "move" in Plato's defense of souls' having the ability to at least partially move themselves (CA; 150). For Plato, the future and generality are two aspects of the same basic mode of reality (WM; 7). The lack of complete order in the world is explained by there being many souls. These many self-active agents imply indefinitely great—if not complete—disorder, unless there is a "supreme soul to 'persuade' the many lesser souls to conform to a cosmic plan. They cannot completely fit such a plan for then they would not be self-determined." That is,

Hartshorne's theodicy, including a notion as to why animals suffer, is essentially Platonic because the divine plan cannot be completely definite and detailed (WV; 23). "God has power over us" has meaning only if we return to Plato's notion of a self-moved mover of others which is also partially moved by these other self-movers. God can "rule the world" by setting optimal limits for free action. Omnipotent power would therefore be a monoply of power over the powerless; but Hartshorne agrees with Plato's claim that being *is* power, hence "to be an individual is to decide" (IO; 367).

Like a child begging for both, Plato declares in the *Sophist* (249D) that reality (as dynamic power) is at once both the unchangeable and that which changes. In this dyadic reality can be distinguished a thing's abstract "essence" from its being-in-a-context-of-relations. Because our knowledge itself is relational, we can never *fully* know the essence of a thing, only an endless series of relations. This intimates how Plato still retains in the later dialogues the notion of separation *(chorismos)*. Hartshorne especially likes to use these Platonic insights to illustrate the aesthetic core of reality in that an individual—cellular or animal—is a functional unity-in-diversity, "so long as it endures at all." Plato's basic idea of beauty of integrated diversity and intensity of experience is truly metaphysical: "valid for any possible state of reality" (CS; 307-308). Dipolarity can be traced back to Plato, and this dipolarity is manifest in all reality, supremely so in God (PS; 2, 5).

For the sake of argument, Hartshorne would drop his thesis regarding phases of Platonic development, but he refuses to give up the thesis that there are two facets in Plato's thought (PS; 39-40, 43). The first is a diaeresis of existence into the quantitative and the qualitative, the mutable and the immutable, or better, the material and the formal (or ideational). Both soul and God are put at the latter (immobile) pole of these pairs. However, in the second facet (or phase) of Plato's thought, motion is granted to both soul and God. The "real opposition" here is between dependent and independent mobility, that is, between body (taken as an insentient aggregate of sentient constituents) and soul (including animal and divine soul). *Within* the World Soul there is a principle of immutability, a principle that characterizes soul per se in the first facet or phase.

Hartshorne views Plato not only as a dipolar theist, but also as a panentheist, such that all is *in* God (PS; 17). There are two principles upon which Plato's theology turns: the "pure being" of the forms and the "supreme mobility" of soul (PS; 54). The unchanging deity of the *Phaedo, Republic,* and *Parmenides* is the supreme instance of fixity; the self-moving deity of the *Phaedrus* and the *Laws* is the supreme instance of mobility. Alluding to the passage in the *Sophist* (to the effect that Plato, like an entreating child, says, "Give us both"), Hartshorne claims that the two poles of Plato's theism are brought together with almost equal weight in the *Timaeus*.

Monotheism is close to the surface of Plato's approach in that God is not posited by Plato as a mere fact to explain some other observed facts; rather, God must comprehend the *entire* realm of forms, for God is the very principle of order in the world, the means by which the totality of things is one cosmos, a *uni*-verse.

The two "Gods" of the *Timaeus* (the creator God and the created God—the Demiurge and the World Soul, respectively) are aspects of one and the same deity. The *uni*verse as an *animate* and rational effect is superior to all other effects "as the whole or inclusive effect is superior to parts or included effects." (DR; 79-80)

Process theology in general "can be regarded as a partial return to Plato," his World Soul as the divine self-moved, but not unmoved, mover of all other self-movers, and as the soul aware of all things. That is, the three sorts of sentiency treated above can be found in Plato as well as in Wordsworth and Hartshorne. In the *Republic* (462C–D) Plato makes it clear that, if there is pain in one's finger (note, not the whole hand), the entire community *(pasa he koinonia)* of bodily connections is hurt; the organized unity of the individual is such that, when one part is hurt, there is a feeling of pain in the whole *(hole)* man who has the pain in his finger (MV; 153). Plato shares with Hartshorne the already mentioned four-term analogy:

$$S1 : S2 :: S2 : S3$$

The universe is a society or an organism (a Platonic World Soul) of which one member (God or the Platonic Demiurge) is preeminent, just as human beings or animals are societies of cells, of which the mental part is preeminent.

Because animal individuals must, to maintain their integrity, adapt to their environment, mortality is implied. But if we imagine the World Soul, we must not consider an environment external to deity, but an internal one: the world body of the world mind. This cosmic, divine animal has such an intimate relation to its body that it must also have ideal ways of perceiving and remembering its body such that it can identify the microindividuals (S2) it includes. We can only tell when cells in our toe have been burned by the fire; we cannot identify the microindividuals as such (IO; 30, 366). It is true that the Demiurge is hampered by necessity *(anangke)* in the effort to conform the world or the contents of the receptacle to the ideal. Yet the Demiurge is not impeded by an environment external to deity, but by a plurality of self-movers. The value of contrast and richness provided by "cosmic 'creativity'" also provides the "recalcitrance of the 'material' ," just as there is the "familiar difficulty of eliciting harmony among a plurality of creatures each having its own freedom." Although the evidence from Plato is somewhat unclear as to how matter "could consist of multitudinous 'souls' of extremely subhuman kinds," and as to how the order of the universe could be a static good forever (which Hartshorne thinks is impossible), Plato had at least a glimmering "that it was the multiplicity of souls that made absolute order impossible" (CS; 116).

Hartshorne has taken the World Soul as a clue for present philosophizing. For example, each new divine state harmonizes itself both with its predecessor and with the previous state of the cosmos. This is analogous to a human being or animal harmonizing itself with its previous experience and bodily state, but with a decisive difference. The human being must hope that its internal and external environment will continue to make it possible for it to survive, whereas God has no such problem in that there is no external environment for God. (AD; 293) But the differences between God and human beings or animals—for example, God knows the microindividuals included in the divine life and God has no external environment—should not cloud the important similarities—for example, the facts that self-change is integral to soul at all levels and that the soul–body analogy used to understand God does not preclude the person–person analogy, which links the divine person with human beings. The most important similarity lies in the fact that one's bodily cells are associated, at a given moment, with one's being a conscious, supercellular singular, just as all lesser beings are associated with the society of singulars called God. (CA; 203, 251, 274) In a way, all talk about God short of univocity contains *some* negativity, in that God does not exist, know, love, etc., exactly as we do. With regard to the divine body, however, almost all theists have allowed this negativity to run wild. (MV; 180) Hartshorne's use of Plato is an attempt to remedy this imbalance.

Plato offered a "striking anticipation" of the doctrine of the compound animal individual, even if he ultimately fell short of the principle that individuality as such must be the compounding of organisms into organisms; but this is not surprising, because cells were not yet discovered (WP; 53-54). In the case of the divine individual, where all entities are fully enjoyed, there can be no envy of others or conflict with them, in that they are integral to the divine goodness. Less completely are an animal's cells internal to the individual; for example, bone cells in a leg are less internal and less fully possessed by the individual than are the brain cells.

These considerations regarding divine inclusiveness also explain why the cosmos could not be held together and ordered by a malevolent God or a plurality of gods, in that these deities are always partly divided within or among themselves, and are incapable of objective grasp of the forms. The cosmos can be held together only by an all-sympathetic coordinator. (RP; 138, 190)

Plato also came closer than any other philosopher to Hartshorne's notion that God is whole in "every categorial sense, all actuality in one individual actuality, and all possibility in one individual potentiality," albeit tempered by Hartshorne's own understanding of the potentiality inherent in God, somewhat less extensive than that found in Whitehead's view. And because of this wholeness God is not an organism of a loose kind which must await the light years it takes for cosmic interactions to take place, in that these interactions are all internal to the divine "ideal animal" itself. (NT; 21, 99)

One of the reasons Hartshorne thinks of Plato as among the "wisest and best" of theologians is that he thinks Plato may have realized that the Demiurge *is* the World Soul in abstraction, that is, is that part of the World Soul considered as having an eternal ideal that it is forever engaged in realizing. This process of realization is what Pluto meant in the *Timaeus* by the "moving image of eternity." Hartshorne's tempting way of reading Plato alleges that God, utilizing partly self-created creatures, "creates its own forever unfinished actualization." Thus, God is aware of both us and other noncosmic animals and lesser souls, on the one hand, and eternal ideals, on the other. Even though God is the "individual integrity" of the world, which is otherwise a concatenation of myriad parts, Hartshorne's view is easily made compatible with the claim that God does not survey all events in the future with strict omniscience. (OO; 52-53, 59, 94)

Belief in a World Soul is connected in the divine animal with a belief in a world body, which is superior to our bodies because there is nothing internal to it (for example, cancer cells) that could threaten its continued existence, even if the divine body is spatially finite. Further, our bodies are fragmentary, as in a human infant's coming into the world as a secondary life style expressing its feelings upon a system that already had a basic order among its cells; whereas the divine body exists on a foundation everlastingly established. When an animal dies, its individual life style no longer controls its members, yet the result is not chaos, but, as before, "simply a return to the more pervasive types of order expressive of the cosmic mind-body." The World Soul is aware of the divine body, and can vicariously suffer with its suffering members, but it cannot suffer in the sense of ceasing to exist due to an alien force. "An individual can influence it, none can threaten it." Not even brain death can threaten it, because the soul–body analogy cannot be pushed to the point where a divine brain is posited. As before, the contrast between the brain and a less essential bodily part only makes sense because an animal has an external environment. Consider that the divine body does not need limbs to move about, for it is its own place: "space being merely the order among its parts." It does not need a digestive system or lungs to take in food or air from outside in that there is no "outside." So it is with all organs outside the central nervous system, which, as we know but Plato did not, is the organ that adapts "internal activities to external stimuli," a function which is not needed in the inclusive organism.[3] The only function of the divine body is to furnish the World Soul with awareness of, and power over, its bodily members. So although there is no special part of the cosmos recognizable as a nervous system, every individual becomes, *as it were,* a brain cell directly communicating to the World Soul, and likewise receiving influences from divine feeling or thought. (OO; 133-135; IO; 348)

These thoughts on the divine body are not just consequences of Hartshorne's use of the soul–body analogy to understand God; they are also logically entailed by his metaphysics. Hartshorne has often claimed (contra Kant et al.) that there are necessary truths concerning existence, for example, "Something exists." Particular animal bodies can pass out of existence (or better, pass into another sort of existence), but the divine body of the universe itself has no alternative but to exist, as is implied in the ontological argument.

If the good is a necessary feature or idea in God, then God for Plato may well be absoluteness necessarily existent somehow, but with the particular actuality of God as both contingent and relative. God's bare *existence* is quite abstract, about as noncompetitive as "reality as such." It has an infinite range of variations and flexibility. But God is not characterless or "flabby," because of God's *actuality* in some embodied state, hence the importance of the divine animal metaphor. The definitive functions of deity are strictly universal and coextensive with modality as such: God is related actually to all actual things and potentially to all potential things. God—à la the *Sophist*—is influenced by and influences everything. Thus, modal coextensiveness is equivalent to the notion of the unsurpassable. The mistake of "Platonism" in the bad sense is the notion that all beautiful things must preexist in the Absolute Form of Beauty, an ultimate determinable that somehow issued in determinations. But this is to deny any intelligible creativity, divine or creaturely.

Although Plato came too close to identifying disorder and evil (for Hartshorne partial disorder is needed to balance order so as to produce beauty), his wisdom is seen when Hume and Kant suggest that the disorder in the world might be explained polytheistically. This is an extreme and inadequate way to put Plato's very point, if by "gods" is meant souls. And we have already seen why order cannot be explained by divine committee. One further reason for this claim needs to be stated here. The higher the consciousness, the more "widely and abruptly" it can disagree with other consciousnesses that are its peers, therefore, a pantheon of gods would be even more in need of a single superior to understand the world as a cosmos than a plurality of earthly animals would.

Souls are not completely self-moved. That they are *also* moved from outside themselves is suggested in the *Symposium* (200–201), in that love implies deficiency of, and admiration for, absolute beauty. But absolute beauty, if this is the union of all possible values, is impossible because there are incompossibles. Positive values are competitive with one another, as in artistic creation, for if one paints in an abstract expressionist style, one cannot at the same time paint as a cubist. Furthermore, aesthetic value is logically incapable of an unsurpassable maximum: there can be a factual maximum of all actual variety ideally integrated, but this can always be surpassed. Hence, the sense in which love in the *Symposium* implies imperfection is not too bothersome if the "perfection" to which it is compared is logically impossible (IO; 28-29.

The Greeks in general had difficulty in conceiving love as divine (or perfect) in itself. When Plato views God as being willing to have others enjoy the blessings of existence, he came close to this conception (NT; 14-15). God "charms every creature irresistibly to whatever extent is compatible with that creature's level of freedom." This is another way of saying that God loves each creature better than each can love God, and this because the highest intrinsic value must be the value of the most perfect and inclusive type of love. Even if Plato did not fully appreciate the divinity of love, Hartshorne thinks it is clear that he got closer to this notion than the medieval theologians (OO; 81, 125). For example, Plato realized that tragedy could not be prevented by an "omnipotent" God, but that this cave of a world could be made bearable and given whatever beauty it is capable of. The refined Platonic conception of love does not see it as the search for supreme beauty; in its highest human and divine varieties it simply *is* that beauty (RP; 108). Divine "love" means divine "relativity" in the concrete aspect of deity (WP; 169), but even the abstract aspect of God illustrates divine persuasive love because one of the exhibitions of divine power is the worship God inspires. Abstractly conceived, the good *is* love, as Plato almost knew (CA; 112, 273). In this abstract sense Plato's notion of beauty in the *Symposium* is instructive: it is the beauty of the perfect abstraction, and as an abstraction it has no defect. But because it is an abstraction it is not the all-inclusive value, it is "only the eternal standard and principle of possible achievements of value, not any actual achievement" (EA; 76-77). Plato was correct that this principle cannot be love, even if it is the abstract principle of the universe besouled, a Wordsworthian World Soul, whose love is cosmic and superhuman.[4]

Hartshorne's (Platonic) panpsychism insists that the notion of being cannot be separated from that of experience; experience is not merely a bridge to reality, it is the paradigm case of reality. Add to this the (Platonic) notion that experience (especially knowing) cannot be separated from value, and we can see why the form of the good is in one sense "ultimate." (CS; 26-27, 70; WP; 173) The ultimate structure of experience is social, in that experience is united either in animal bodies or in the divine body, as Plato vaguely saw (DR; 28). This Platonic metaphysics of social structure can be cited along with other reasons in the attempt to deemphasize a pretentious theory of self-interest (found, but not emphasized, in Plato), which suggests that a "rational ethics depends upon the possibility of showing that the good man is bound to be benefitted in the long run by his own good acts." (Philo agrees with Plato that the selfish person is the fickle one as well—PS; 81). If there is no *uni*verse, no World Soul to bring the world together into a social (animate) structure, then the atheistic virtue of courage, as opposed to love, in the face of the distant doom of humanity seems "childish." In fact, this is not courage *(andreia)*, but what Plato would call folly *(anoias—Laches* 197). If love is the heightening of internal relations among beings that care for each other, then love must ultimately be grounded in God, who is internally related to all beings: this is why God, for Plato and Hartshorne, is the proper object of worship (CS; 202, 261; BH; 16; CA; 230).

Hartshorne's recent work in the history of philosophy, as well as his previous work (especially PS), makes it clear that Plato is the standard against which all philosophical progress and regress is to be measured, starting with his great pupil Aristotle. My purpose here is not to outline Hartshorne's views on the history of philosophy, but to show how such an outline almost always requires Plato as a model.

The divine in Aristotle is far more eternalist than in Plato, and resembles Plato's form of the good because it is like a magnet operating from an armchair.[5] Aristotle's stress on the eternalistic side of Plato was continued by Philo, Plotinus, and most of the medieval thinkers. That is, Aristotle paid insufficient attention to the mind–body analogy for God, and to the doctrine that soul is self-moved. It is not surprising that God for him was not a person.

Hartshorne thinks that Aristotle in some ways did improve on Plato, and not necessarily because of his notion of embodied form, as many would suppose. For example, Aristotle seems to deny personal immortality, and he was the first to explicitly state that what comes to be is contingent. Surprisingly, however,

Aristotle failed to relate this insight to the life of an individual, which he connected with a notion of substantial personhood, a substance that remained the same from birth to death. Unfortunately, his substances still stroll the world, as do his speciesism and sexism, both of which were largely avoided by Plato. As with many other questions, Plato carefully read tends to correct Aristotle's mistakes. (OO; 8, 54, 77-78, 104)

None of this is meant to deny certain similarities between Plato and Aristotle: both believed that the soul "ruled" the body, and both underemphasized how bodily members act upon the soul (NT; 97). Although Plato had more of a mathematical bent than Aristotle, who had more of a taste for biology, both saw that there is a metaphysical element in knowledge, in which they often —not always— exaggerated a contempt for becoming. (Only Heraclitus in the ancient world clearly held the primacy of becoming, in Hartshorne's view.) Plato partially escaped from this contempt with his later doctrine on soul as self-moved; Aristotle apparently remained fixed in his notion that change was due to the combination of mind with matter. Hence, Hartshorne thinks, Plato was a better physicist than Aristotle, and not only because Plato believed there was (contra Aristotle) divine knowledge of individuals: Plato avoided Aristotle's troublesome ambiguity on localized substances by analyzing change as successive qualifications of the cosmic receptacle, even if Plato was somewhat unclear about the extent to which chance operates in the receptacle. However, at times Plato gives the indication that he is a dualist, implying along with Aristotle that there are at least some unbesouled entities. Plato's more sophisticated view tends toward psychical monism. His tentativeness here is nonetheless part of his genius, superior in Hartshorne's view to Aristotle's "confident air of proving his answers," which well suited the medieval temper. (IO; xiv, 19, 40, 70-72, 365)

Before leaving Aristotle, the point should be reiterated that for both Plato (though not for Platonism) and Aristotle the abstract must somehow be embodied in concrete actuality. For Plato, this embodiment is in God's thoughts. For Aristotle it is either *in re* (embodied in a material thing) or *post rem* (abstracted in the mind of a knower). So for Plato and Aristotle no particular concrete entity is required by the abstract entity. "A necessarily instantiated attribute could be clearly nonidentical with its instances, and yet in its very being, as an attribute, instantiated somehow" (AD; 289). But there is a difference of emphasis in the two thinkers, with Aristotle developing a single categorial scheme of substance, in place of Plato's dipolarity. Paradoxically, however, from this emphasis on substance, Aristotle ultimately constructs a more vicious dualism than any ever envisaged by Plato, in that Aristotle's divinity is a completely self-sufficient entity separated from all change and multiplicity. Painting with a rather wide brush, Hartshorne's view seems to be that Plato's cosmology of psychical monism can only be understood and explained through a dipolar categorial scheme, as seen above, whereas Aristotle's troublesome cosmological dualism is elaborated through a monopolar scheme favoring substance and eternality (PS; 58-59).

The Greeks—Plato, Aristotle, and Epicurus among them—realized that any possible world must involve a multiplicity of individuals, each making their own decisions, hence there is an aspect of real chance in what happens (OO; 15). Unfortunately this notion of chance was not sufficiently synthesized by Plato with the (materialistic) atomism of Leucippus and Democritus (IO; 16). It is perhaps this failure which accounts for the monopolarity of the neo-platonists in their interpretation of Plato.

For example, in a way, Plotinus reaffirms Plato's "three aspects of the ultimate" in the *Timaeus*: the forms (especially the form of the good), the Demiurge, and the World Soul. These appear in Plotinus as the One, Intellect or *Nous,* and the Plotinian World Soul. But Plotinus has a (necessitarian) logical principle for the progression from the One to the World Soul. Plotinus's ontolatry differs from Plato's World Soul because the self-motion of soul is replaced by a conception of soul with a merely "accidental and superficial motility," a motility derived in an Aristotelian way from body rather than from the soul's own nature. Plotinus at least enhanced Plato's aesthetic argument for God, and he rightly viewed Plato's forms as essentially "objects-for-*Nous,*" but for the most part his monopolarity detracted from an appreciation of Plato's greatest insights. (PS; 211-212, 221) Hartshorne finds it "comic" to watch Plotinus trying to prove that without unity and simplicity we cannot understand the multiple and complex. How true!, but without plurality, contrast, and complexity there is "no unity, beauty, goodness, value, or reality." (CS; 121)

Plato was as close as the ancient Greek world got to panentheism, just as the Hindu thinker Ramanuja was as close as ancient India got, but neither world made this position a live issue for over a thousand years. Ramanuja would agree with Plato's insight that body is in soul, and not vice versa; that is, subjectivity is more inclusive than objectivity. (PS; 188) Tertullian followed Plato somewhat in asserting a world body (OO; 53), but Hartshorne constantly criticizes the dominant medieval view, based on "pseudo-platonic simplifications" of terms like absolute, infinite, and immutable (NT; 28). "Whereas Plato had at least a glimmering of the modern concept of self-creativity as inherent in experience or mind as such, Aristotle (or Plotinus, or a few texts in the Bible) misled the Scholastics into rejecting this concept" (IO; 75). And although Descartes is described by Hartshorne as "the Moses of Modern Philosophy," in many ways he continued the medieval tradition. The slogan, "events, not things," makes the distinction between mind and matter less and less relevant, but it is precisely this distinction that Descartes takes as ultimate, hence for Hartshorne he was stuck with some misconstrued "Platonic" notions (IO; 113).

The real break with classical theism was provided by Spinoza and Faustus Socinus. The former had some notion of World Soul, but his denial of freedom in God and creatures makes the notion unintelligible (OO; 122).[6] A more meaningful break was provided by Socinus, the first philosopher for almost two thousand years to develop a conception of God akin to that found in the *Timaeus* (although, for Hartshorne, Cicero and William of Occam also came close to such a conception). There are at least three doctrinal possibilities: no God; a wholly immutable God; a God not wholly immutable. Socinus was the first philosopher after Plato to consistently and seriously consider the third option (IO; 2, 375).

Yet of all of the philosophers in the modern period, it is Leibniz who most captivates Hartshorne. Leibniz (along with Plato, Peirce, and Whitehead) is in the pantheon of Hartshorne's greatest philosophical influences; hence he has exerted a greater influence on Hartshorne than any other of the classical theists. It is no accident that all four of these great philosophical influences were mathematicians, for Hartshorne's method always rests upon a logicaly exhaustive table of alternative positions (CS; xvii). But all philosophers for Hartshorne, Plato and Leibniz among them, are careful only on some questions, confused on others (CA; 208); Leibniz's greatness stems from being extremely careful on several issues. For example, Leibniz's distinction between singular acting agents and aggregates of those agents improves on Plato's inability to fully understand the animal individual and to carry through his cosmological scheme. That is, although a classical theist, Leibniz was the first philosopher to enable us to carry through "the genuinely Platonic program" of the later dialogues; to explain all process through psychical process. Even today the alternative to this view is materialism, as Plato and Leibniz (opponents in different ways to dualism) said it was. Thus, Hartshorne thinks that if philosophy of nature has a future, it will lie in a "modernized Platonism," of which Leibniz was, paradoxically, the best and the worst example. He largely missed Plato's notion of creativity, and Leibniz's concepts of sufficient reason and theodicy are defective in many ways, according to Hartshorne's interpretation (IO; 132-133).

Even as brilliant a thinker as Kant succumbed to the supposedly "platonist" conception that God's uniqueness lies in exhaustively actualizing possible value, which, as we have seen, Hartshorne thinks is impossible. Rather, there is no consistent set of possible values that God could not enjoy. *This* is the divine uniqueness, whereas Kant's version of the true divine ideal has nothing to do with self-surpassable but otherwise unsurpassable creativity (AD; 218).[7]

Hartshorne is tentative on the influence of Plato on Hegel. Plato saw that multiple freedom means partial disorder, even though "freedom must be given ordering directives from supreme or divine freedom to enable it to accomplish anything." If this is Hegel's view, then, on Hartshorne's assumptions regarding the virtue of clarity, Hegel should have said so more forthrightly so as to make clear his debt to Plato on this point. (IO; 211)

Schopenhauer is more explicitly a follower of the divine Plato *(der Gottliche Platon)*, whose forms allowed Schopenhauer a Buddhist-like escape from suffering and from becoming, just as in Plato's *Seventh Letter.* Although Hartshorne would disagree with the concept that becoming is necessarily evil, he would agree that, in contemplating the eternal, we achieve a kind of "peace or partial respite from the restless striving in which we tend to be immersed" (IO; 190-191). Kierkegaard makes an allied point, maintained in a confused way by Plato, that a human individual's career is not finally a topic for science, but for faith (IO; 213). As with the neoplatonists and medieval philosophers, however, the Platonism of Kant, Kierkegaard, and Friedrich von Hügel was of a monopolar sort (PS; 153, 162).

As in the case of Socinus in the sixteenth century, Hartshorne often sees great philosophical progress having been made by relatively obscure figures compared to better known philosophers. "Progress" here is largely synonymous with what we have previously seen Hartshorne refer to as "the genuinely Platonic program." In the nineteenth and early twentieth centuries several thinkers (Jules Lequier, Bernardino Varisco, Mohammed Iqbal) returned to Platonic, panenthestic notions. Otto Pfleiderer actually argues for the ubiquity of deity in the shape of Plato's ideal animal (IO; 251). Hartshorne especially admires the thought of Fechner, who

> was not another Plato; yet no one between Plato and Fechner was able to affirm of God with such clarity and forcefulness the full range of themes common to . . . these two philosophers. Indeed, Fechner at his best advanced the view of an inclusive eternal-temporal deity far beyond the point which Plato at his best had reached.

Fechner also agreed with Plato that God's environment was internal and that change occurs through change in the self-changing principle itself. (PS; 243; OO; 122).

The relation between Plato and American philosophers also impresses Hartshorne. Even Jonathan Edwards' notion of beauty as order is Platonic in its own way, although hampered by his neoplatonic and Calvinist bias. Hartshorne's own theory of beauty encourages both the avoidance of mere order or unity as much as the avoidance of randomness or diversity, as we will see in the next chapter in connection with bird song. Peirce called Josiah Royce "our American Plato," a label which has its justification in his "keen awareness of mathematical and logical structures, his eloquence, and lofty vision of human and superhuman actualities" (CA; 24, 72). But the same designation could almost as well be applied to Peirce (or Hartshorne!) himself: both Plato and Peirce were astonishingly inventive; both could coax insights from many different subjects; neither thinker yields easily to a single structure or a single interpretation; and scholars of both thinkers disagree as to whether there is any unity—explicit or implicit—in their philosophic works.

Although the connections between Plato and James are not as tight as those of Plato with Peirce, Hartshorne is nonetheless confident that James, more than anyone except Plato, "was the psychologist of the philosophical mind" (PS; 258, 335). George Santayana was obviously a Platonic realist; not so obvious (but nonetheless persuasive, I think) is Hartshorne's claim that Santayana's realism is much more extreme than we need suppose Plato's to have been. This extreme Platonic realism, passed down from Santayana to W.P. Montague, "takes rather too little into account Plato's more mature dialogues." And E.S. Brightman comes close to solving Plato's problem in the *Euthyphro* as to how to understand "God is good" if "good" is defined as divinely commanded (CA; 114, 203, 211).

It should now be obvious that Hartshorne's use of Plato as a heuristic device to understand the history of philosophy is not at all like the procedure of Heidegger, whom Hartshorne heard teach the history of philosophy backward: from Edmund Husserl to Descartes, from Descartes to the scholastics, from the scholastics to Aristotle, from Aristotle to Plato and the presocratics. "The moral seemed to be that the first persons to have an idea were clearest about the intuitive evidences without which the idea tends to lose much of its meaning." Hartshorne's view more resembles a roller coaster, with both progress and regress possible, "progress" often, but not always, meaning the regaining of lost (Platonic) ground. This progress is often achieved in piecemeal fashion by attacking isolated problems in Plato, particularly the problem of God in the later dialogues (IO; xv).

No one in the history of philosophy embodies this progress better than Whitehead, who also has an intimate relation to Plato (IO; xiii), but no more intimate, I allege, than Hartshorne's. Whitehead came to philosophy as Plato thought one should—but as English Platonists like Wordsworth have not done—through mathematics and reflection on the good, although Whitehead's formal logic is a splendid tool that Plato did not have. One of the purposes to which Whitehead directed his skills was understanding of God; his illuminating doctrine of God as primordial and necessary as well as consequent and contingent is an elaboration of Plato's own accounts of God, or better, is a return to Plato after a long detour. Whitehead also learned from Plato that it is the divine beauty that moves the world, not omnipotence, (WP; 6, 54, 154; OO; 14, 53, WV; 2, 12; PS; 276). Hence, Plato, Whitehead, and Hartshorne would argue for a "dice-throwing God." Einstein's rejection of this notion was "a great man's error." Note that human beings and animals are some—indeed the most important—of the dice.

Whitehead is the only twentieth-century philosopher, in Hartshorne's view, to recall Plato to "any striking degree" with respect to the ideas that ordinary, surpassable forms of creativity in their multiplicity explain why disorder and conflict exist, while extraordinary, unsurpassable creativity in its ubiquity explains how the disorders and frustrations can be contained within a basic order, just as irrational numbers can be cajoled and used within an overall orderliness in geometry. Whitehead (along with Peirce) pushes "the genuinely Platonic program" further in a significant way, for the first time after Leibniz, in that singular individuals (including animal individuals) and aggregates are explained in greater detail than before, as is the receptacle or space. (NT; 113-115; MV; 28).

Further, Hartshorne defends Whitehead against Karl Popper's charge that in social philosophy he was a collectivist.[8] Whitehead (Plato too?) was only committed to the idea that morality is inseparably conjoined with generality of outlook (IO; 307). Obviously this praise of Whitehead's Platonism should not be taken as a panegyric to either Plato or Whitehead, because Hartshorne criticizes both thinkers on several serious points. As before, Hartshorne agrees with Nicolas Berdyaev that Whitehead's eternal objects are too "Platonic" because they threaten the truth that creation is the "production of new images," not the mere actualization of eternal patterns. Perhaps one can say that for Hartshorne and Berdyaev only creativity itself is a transcendental or eternal object (WP; 186-187).

From Hartshorne's early encounter with the Platonism of Emerson, to his doctoral dissertation in 1923 (where Plato is cited as "the great founder" of Hartshorne's own teleological monism and monistic principle [9]), to all of his books throughout his career, especially his works after CS in 1970 (which are also the works, not coincidentally, where Hartshorne most fully develops his thought on animals), Hartshorne has been in the process of trying to understand and, where necessary, improve upon Plato. Yet how odd it is that Hartshorne has to remind even a thinker as familiar with his work as Cobb of the importance of Plato for his idea of God. I hope we are now in a position, however, to take Hartshorne seriously when he says in 1984 that: "I have always been something of a Platonist" (EA; 164-165).

Chapter Eight

The Aesthetic Analogy

The rapture of the Hallelujah sent
From all that breathes and is,
was chasten'd, stemm'd
And balanced by a Reason which indeed
Is reason; duty and pathetic truth . . . .
Drunken lark! . . .
With a soul as strong as a mountain river
Pouring out praise to the almighty Giver.

Whereas Chapters Six and Seven have examined the heart of Hartshorne's thought, this chapter looks at its surface, its skin; or better, this chapter entertains the sound of Hartshorne's thought, which resonates from its Platonic depths. That is, the aesthetic analogy between human beings and animals (particularly the songs of birds) can only be understood against the background of some basic Platonic categories: unity, diversity, and intensity of experience.

An explanation of nature is usually considered better if, other things being equal, it is simpler. Partly because of this aesthetic ideal, behaviorism poses itself as a plausible form of intellectual parsimony: a higher function, remote from the beginnings of life, is not needed if a more primitive function can account for the matter in question. Hartshorne has no objection to the "principle of parsimony," but he is bothered by the suggestion that behaviorism is equal in explanatory power to psychicalism (BS; 1). As Whitehead put it, seek simplicity and then distrust it. For example, in selecting for behavior, evolution may be indirectly selecting for modes of feeling that promote such behavior (WM; 108).

Unfortunately, many believe that aesthetic ideals only concern subordinate refinements of life and not the central issues. Relying on Peirce, Hartshorne believes that this less than exalted view of aesthetic phenomena is due to a failure to generalize concepts like harmony, feeling, and unity in variety (BS; 2). A satisfactory account (contra behaviorism) of human beings and other animals would have to notice that all animal activity is motivated by a sense of harmony and by the flight from two evils: discord and monotony. As before, moral or ethical values are not universal because animals cannot exhibit them; aesthetic values are universal (WM; 52).

Human aesthetic responses are beyond those of animals, but this is not because they are aesthetic, rather because they are pervaded by an intellectual element. Aesthetic feeling is not the same as aesthetic thought; animals certainly have the former. They are curious, and the sexual behavior they need to exhibit to survive through evolutionary process is not just behavior: it also gives them pleasure. Sexual behavior is a mode of feeling as well as a mode of acting, (BS; 3).

Even if it is granted that the primary function of bird song is to "maintain territory," why must this be taken to mean that the bird is hostile, or that the bird can exclusively be described in the behaviorist's terms? Why not just as legitimately say that the bird *likes* its territory? Or why not say the bird, at least part of the time, finds joy in singing? Members of military bands can also enjoy their music. And human beings make love for reasons other than the production of offspring (WM; 110). Is it not incredible to believe that bird feelings are epiphenomena? Think of avoidance of painful burns. And when a bird sits on eggs, it does so not just out of "instinct," but also because of the enjoyment involved. (EA; 186; MN; 91) Early in the reproductive season, blackbirds' songs are largely functional, but later, according to W.H. Thorpe, they turn into music.[1] Or as Whitehead has it concerning one of Aesop's fables: a dog is on the road towards a free imagination. The fable has it that a dog with food in its mouth saw its reflection in water, where the food looked twice as big; it went after the larger portion, losing what it had. But aesthetically it had gained a great deal. "Evolutionary causes of present behavior lie deep in the past, but the animal is living now" (BS; 3).

Bird song is affected by certain male hormones, such that it is maximal at breeding season; but these physical factors alter not just the behavior but also the feelings of the bird. "The notion that emotions are mere 'idle wheels,' or epiphenomena, is suspect" (BS; 4). Two extremes are to be avoided: ignoring animal feelings altogether and swelling them into "anthropomorphic orgies" (BS; 4). Hartshorne tries to find a reasonable mean between these two. He is aided in this effort by Peirce's distinction between physics and psychics. (MN; 89-91) The former deals with an animal's spatio-temporal-causal properties, while the latter, the more inclusive discipline, deals with how and why an animal feels and intends. Thus, we have a dual access to animate reality, with psychics enabling us to use animals—without anthropomorphic excess—in the effort to understand gases, fluids, and minerals, as well as the psychology of single cells. These latter do respond to stimuli and organize their internal activities well, especially single-celled animals and plants. That is, cells resemble entire animals. (GN; 61)

Analogies give thought the power to generalize, and without them thought is relatively powerless; but with them thought is liable to be led astray. Hartshorne cautiously tries to note the analogy between birds and human beings with respect to music (BS; 4). In order to do this, he is required to distinguish between the subjective and objective aspects of aesthetic response. To say of something, "I like it," is not to describe the thing liked. (BS; 6) But to say "I like it because of its unity" is to imply something about the thing. The following diagram displays some of the properties of both human music and bird music-song, treated as objects, properties that human beings, at least, can become aware of:

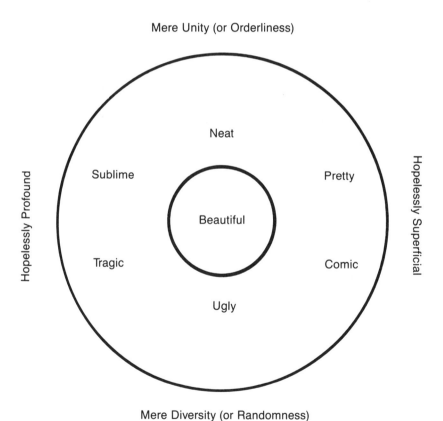

Not all of music is beautiful although beauty is the central aesthetic value (BS; 6). Beauty is central because it is a mean between two sets of extremes. On the one hand, it is between mere unity (or orderliness) and mere diversity (or randomness). Running up the scale of notes chromatically is neat but not beautiful, because its orderliness is too great. Yet since freedom entails limits as well as indeterminacy, mere diversity is not beautiful either, and can cause cacophony. Beauty lies between hopeless superficiality and profound complexity. Prettiness is superficial beauty, whereas sublimity is beauty made extraordinarily intense. A little flower is simple, whereas a well-designed garden or a natural forest is profound (WM; 2). Obviously, deviations from the mean have great aesthetic worth, especially the tragic complexity of profound figures like Lear. Only hopelessly unfree (merely unified), hopelessly chaotic, hopelessly simple (hence trivial), or hopelessly overcomplicated (and hence unintelligible) sounds are without aesthetic worth. (BS; 7)

The word "hopeless," however, is relative to a given species or a given organism. That is, there are no absolute rules for applying these categories, which must remain heuristic devices rather than algorithmic assurances. What is complex or profound for a bird is probably ultrasimple for a human being. What is ordered for a human being is probably chaos for a bird. Even among human beings there are differences. For example, nature lovers find coffee plantations dull compared to a rain forest (WM; 38). Complete relativity, however, does not follow. Higher organisms can have at least some sympathy and understanding for lower types, particularly for their feelings. Unfortunately, the reverse relation does not seem possible for most animals, although dogs have been known to risk their own lives for their masters'.[2] Some animals enjoy our music.

In the above diagram the region outside the larger circle represents "zero aesthetic value" for a given organism (BS; 8). Inside the larger circle are aesthetic values; even ugliness has some of this in that it acts as a stimulus. (Hunters are prone to exploit this fact by claiming that because nature is inherently violent, there is nothing wrong with humans imitating nature. But if some animal herds need to be culled, this should be done reluctantly and painlessly,—for example, through sedative darts—rather than joyfully in an ugly "sport".) Zero aesthetic value is not even ugly, because it is not noticed at all. Beauty, however, is:

> the norm of this achievement equally far from the four extremes or poles of failure—mere disorder, as opposed to mere (lifeless) order; utter triviality as opposed to complexity entirely beyond grasp. All aesthetic value is either

beauty or a not too extreme deviation from it in one of the four directions: toward more chaos *or* lifeless order; toward negligible complexity and intensity *or* baffling complexity, unattainable intensity.

It may be that only a human being can experience contrasts between the beautiful and the pretty, and the like, but this is by no means certain. A recently trapped and caged wild animal (for example, a polar bear) experiences discord to a tragic degree; while after long conditioning to its cage, it accepts dull contentment—"acceptable though not thrilling routine"—which is analogous to human neatness. Playful animals that are excited by some harmless amusement—a kitten with a ball of string—are comic.

Any observer of animals, including birds—perhaps especially birds for Hartshorne, in that he has studied them since he was a boy in Pennsylvania (EA; xiii)—can cite examples of these types of animal response. Bird song, in varying degrees, can have objectively aesthetic properties. Birds, like the wild animal that has recently been trapped, and like human artists, try to approach an ideal balance between "expected repetition and the unexpected, that joint avoidance of monotony and chaos on a sufficient level of complexity, which is beauty" (BS; 9). Even birds are subject to "fatiguing of attention," and they have sensory processes that work to counteract such fatigue and monotony. The thrust of Hartshorne's extensive (and, for the most part, nonphilosophical) work on birds, *Born to Sing,* is that bird songs: (1) indicate the avoidance of both mere regularity (unrelieved by deviations or pauses) and mere randomness; (2) have multifunctional roles, which can appear as sexual drives, youthful play, aesthetic enjoyment, etc.; (3) exhibit, even in the best singers, a limited attention span when compared with human beings—this on the evidence of the shortness of the reiterated unit patterns; and (4) show the presence of both imitativeness and imagination as forms of aesthetic sensitivity (BS; 225-226).[3]

The world itself is beautiful when the happiness of creatures harmonizes under divine influence, although not even God determines such harmony in its concrete particularity. This is a beauty of which every creature catches glimpses, and to which it makes contributions, but only God enjoys it as a whole once it comes into being. (OO; 25) Widely differing species make up the "web of life" (OO; 67), which can only be made ugly by the gaps caused by human beings. Animals killing other animals ensure that beauty is often tragic, but this is not ugliness. The wild sheep of the Rockies did well for thousands of years, despite the wolves who attacked them of necessity, until human beings came along, "civilized" human beings at that. (OO; 130) And we human beings can learn something from birds regarding our monotonous perceptions of male and female roles.

> Taking approximately 9,000 species of birds, we find the following: of the functions or activities that are physiologically possible for both sexes, as nest-building is and egg-laying is not, some are performed by the males in most but not in all species, thus singing or plumage display, and others are performed by females in most but not in all species. No function physically possible for both sexes is reserved exclusively or even primarily for one sex in all species. In some species the male does much more to care for the young than the female—in the uniquely individuated species, humanity, there should be nothing physically possible for women that only men do and nothing physically possible for men that only women do. (GN; 63).

From all of this it follows, Hartshorne thinks, that the aesthetic blindness of modern science, particularly in the case of the behaviorists' treatment of animals, is more than a superficial defect. It makes science less illuminating (that is, less accurate) than it could be. "The scorn of some of our youths for science is not unrelated to this deficiency" (BS; 227). Because Hartshorne himself is now quite old, I assume he means, in Wordsworthian fashion, youthful minds of any age. As pessimists, we might bemoan the loss of the glory and dream of youth, that the aesthetic analogy between human beings and animals might be preserved. But as optimists we might note that what has at one time been, must ever be. It is an incredible fact about nature that:

> the territorial disputes of thousands of species are something like artistic contests—song duels. The struggle is mainly musical (counter-singing), not pugilistic. If only human beings could do so well. (BS; 2-7)

Aesthetic criteria of value are the universal ones; the key to value is not the identity of consciousness with its object, but the "harmony of contrasting feelings." Love (defined before, as delighting in the lives of others) has myriad forms: superhuman, human, subhuman. In the subhuman it is largely love without language; in humans, with language; in God, beyond language. (IO; 201) Love is the interest of experience in other experience, or of subjects in other subjects; Hartshorne's view here is close to Peirce's agapism (IO; 320). Through love, or, if you will, sympathy, the world receives its solidarity. Erazim Kohàk puts the key choice as follows:

> Shall we conceive of the world around us and of ourselves in it as *personal,* a meaningful whole, honoring its order as continuous with the moral law of

our own being and its beings as continuous with ours, bearing its goodness—or shall we conceive of it and treat it, together with ourselves, as *impersonal,* a chance aggregate of matter propelled by a blind force and exhibiting at most the ontologically random lawlike regularities of a causal order?[4]

This is the choice we have to make. Hartshorne obviously chooses the first of the two.

God is love, we are told; Hartshorne allows us to make some sense of this. God is also ubiquitous, but the interplay even of various loves can lead to tragedy. The details of the world are not contrived; the *interplay* of free acts itself is largely a matter of chance. (IO; 201) Life not only supports, but also competes with other life; human beings especially compete with each other and other species. Nor is this necessarily bad, since variety, as has been seen, is an aesthetic good, and not only for human beings, but for God and animals as well. But variety has its price: a rich man can keep a forest, but a poor man can understandably desire to cut it down for firewood (IO; 224). "Caprice is an inalienable aspect of all animal existence" (IO; 243); human beings have a special ability to distort their delight in others. Another aesthetic good also has a price: the completion of a life in its beginning, middle, and end. Seen in this light, death simply as such, apart from *when and how* we die, is not in every respect an evil, but can contribute aesthetic value. (IO; 326)

Human love, largely released from the control of instinct, can be comic or tragic (IO; 335); Shakespeare made much of this. But even the tragic extermination of life on this planet (often caused by love of the abstraction "nation") would not destroy the already actualized experiences of animals and human beings, preserved by God's cosmic awareness (IO; 336). Those who are only familiar with Hartshorne's carefully reasoned work on the ontological argument may be surprised at his romanticism and aestheticism, and even more surprised at what appears to be his mysticism. All of these labels have received bad reputations because of inadequate defenders. Mysticism can either mean: (1) immediate experience of God or (2) the belief that this experience and God are ineffable. The first is quite distinct from the second. (MR; 463) It is certainly paradoxical that God could only be affirmed indirectly, especially if God is ubiquitous. We are more like nonintrospective animals than we usually admit. Data that are only sometimes present (for example, red or pain) are easier to detect than those that are always there (for example, S1—microscopic sentiency—or S3—divine sentiency). The mystic is only relatively different from the rest of us: the mystic simply is more *aware* of experiencing what all human beings experience. In this regard only the mystic escapes animal-like

unconsciousness. (MR; 467) "With an eye made quiet by the power of harmony and the deep power of joy," says Wordsworth in "Tintern Abbey," the
mystic sees "into the life of things."

Obviously none of this should be taken to mean that animals are completely unconscious. With animal mind comes a distinctive type of ability to
pass on acquired characteristics, as in song birds teaching new songs to their
young (OO; 84).[5] Over long periods of time a gregarious species like barn
swallows can change considerably. These changes at times even seem to be
desired. "Animals survive partly because they *want* to succeed." (OO; 85)
Although birds do not know what nests are for, they nonetheless feel that a
certain shape is successful. The greater the power of thinking becomes, the less
behavior can be physically determined. Hence in human beings religion is a
biological necessity.[6]

God is aesthetically superior to creatures not because the latter are finite;
God is also finite, at least in one pole of the divine life. If God were not finite
in some sense God could not concretely relate to creatures here and now. Rather,
creatures differ from God because they are *fragmentary,* they do not bring the
world together as a totality. That is, God's aesthetic superiority is connected
with the fact that the mind–body analogy initiated by Plato to describe the
God–World relationship is superior to the sort of analogy used by Aristotle
and the Church Fathers (ruler–subject, parent–child, etc.). Creaturely inferiority, however, does not mean that creatures have no aesthetic wholeness; what
acts as one also feels as one, but what acts as one is often invisible—in plants
it is cells, in stars it is molecules.[7] If Thomas McFarland is correct that the most
important feature of romanticism is its fascination with reticulation or wholeness
as well as with the realization that creatures are diasparactive (from *diasparactos,*
to tear to pieces) fragments of the whole, then Hartshorne's status as a romantic
thinker and his solidarity with nonhuman animals seems secure.[8]

Divine beauty is constituted not only by God's unity, but also by diversity, and not only that diversity which creatures contribute to the divine life.
God's internal nature itself is dual in that, as abstract concepts, each pole in
the divine nature is equal, even if in their application one pole—that is,
becoming—includes its correlative—being. But the more insistent diversity
that helps constitute divine beauty comes from what creatures contribute to
God. Absolute order cannot be guaranteed in the world, not because God is
weak, but because it would not be strength to abolish creaturely freedom; to
do so would make the world incredibly monotonous. The power of selection
among incompatible possibilities is a measure of excellence and is constitutive
of beauty, rather than a deficiency. For example, when a human being selects

a career, opportunities are cut off that an ape could not even consider, while the ape stands in a similar relation to a subanimal being. Unactualized possibilities increase with perfection; the most perfect could hardly equal zero possibility.

Hartshorne is the first great philosopher since Aristotle to also be an ornithologist. It should now be clear how Hartshorne's study of birds has contributed to his philosophy, but his metaphysics has also contributed to ornithology, as several of his reviewers have noted (WM; 105-112, 147). His discovery of a "monotony threshold" in birds is an outgrowth of his philosophy. Repetitive singers (like wood warblers) avoid monotony by the length of pauses between their singing. Versatile singers (like Eurasian skylarks) usually use few pauses. And some species exhibit variety at dawn or evening without pauses, and exhibit repetition the rest of the day with pauses.

The diversity provided to the world by birds makes it obvious why we should study them: they fly and migrate; their warm-bloodedness gives them a quickness and vivacity that is stimulating to behold; they are smaller than we are but not as apparently insignificant as insects; their species are myriad but not so large as to baffle comprehension; they do not harm us; they do not compete with us; they have feathers; they are like us in being primarily guided by sight; and, of course, they sing![9] That is, birds are a happy medium between animals that are too close to us as destructive human beings and animals too remote from us to be easily comprehensible. Birds are wonderfully like and unlike us. Although we can learn moral lessons from birds (for example, how to settle disputes or understand gender roles), this is not the justifying fruit of bird study. Rather, we most gain in aesthetics from the study of birds.

Bird song is an example of prettiness, not sublimity.[10] Its major difference from human music is in its simplicity. The mean between order and disorder in music must be taken temporally, chiefly through a mixture between the expected and unexpected. At one extreme in bird song we have a short song pattern, as in a mere trill or a monotonic repetition, reiterated hundreds or thousands of times a day. Monotony, however, is avoided in the pauses between reiterations, at least if human beings pay attention to these pauses. For the bird, monotony is avoided more easily because of its short memory span. At the other extreme, there are birds who sing contrasting songs and phrases, sometimes fifty or more. These may be reiterated or sung in no predictable order; with repetitive singing, pauses are generally longer than the songs, whereas nonrepetitive singing generally has short pauses, as in the mockingbird or English skylark. Amazingly these phenomena are exactly what the aesthetic (and Platonic) principles call for.

No bird can master a pattern lasting longer than a few seconds, then it must pause, repeat the pattern, or move to a new one. Even parrots and mynas talk in brief sentences. But bird song is recognizably musical by human standards. It has melody, rhythm, harmony (birds, unlike us, can sing contrasting notes simultaneously), theme with variations, accelerando, rallentando, crescendo, diminuendo, interval inversion, even change of key and tempo (as when a trill is given at half or double speed). By contrast, insects have no melody because they cannot discriminate pitches, even if they do have rhythm, which, if human drumming is considered, constitutes a type of music. And their memory span is even shorter than birds, except in insects like cicadas, whose sounds can last thirty seconds. Nonetheless, katydids, like birds, avoid monotony by varying the number of repetitions of a phrase; and batrachians have the beginnings of pitch and hence of melody. But neither batrachians nor insects can compare with birds as musicians. Not even mammals can compare with birds, even though gibbons have songs comparable to a mediocre song bird.

A basic test of musical feeling is to imitate sounds. Song birds almost universally have this tendency. What exactly is the relation between human music and that of its predecessors developed ages ago in insects, frogs, lizards, and birds? Primitive human beings provide us with a clue in that they were far closer than we are to the musical animals. For example, medicine men, who listened to the animals much more than we do, were imputed with magical powers because they could imitate the calls and songs of birds. Comparing bird and human music is justified by more than imitation, however, in that birds are anatomically more fitted for melody and harmony than human beings. That is, the syrinx, the bird's vibrating organ, is not a set of cords in the windpipe but the windpipe itself, like a built-in flute, in which harmonic overtones occur most easily. Only brain limitations prevent birds from doing symphonies. Birds are the only instinctive musicians with any complexity of pattern, as is seen in young birds who play with their music. Yet their music is not merely instinctive, because they improve considerably with practice and imitation.

Thus the real mystery in human beings is not that they make music but that they talk; not even the simple elements of speech are present in birds. The implicit grammatical rules and the mixture of parts of speech are missing. The whole bird song is often an expletive announcing (and rejoicing in) its territory or sex or breeding condition; the parts of the song have no separate meaning. Once recognition is effected, the whole message is conveyed, like understanding a whole Beethovan symphony upon hearing a few of its notes. Because the parts of bird song "have no separate denotative meaning, they can be combined simply in terms of how well they sound together." Birds therefore are quite naturally aesthetic beings.

As already admitted, Hartshorne is open to the charge of anthropomorphism here. But who is really being anthropomorphic? Reacting against the sentimentalism of older naturalists, Aldous Huxley (not Julian) and some ornithologists completely reject the notion that birds offer sweet rhapsodies to God. The new version has the bird suggesting, "Get out or I'll peck your eyes out!" Yet to make this the entire message of bird song seems to mirror too accurately our own violence as human beings. "No known facts conflict with the idea that the bird enjoys its singing. . . . I believe that the older sentimentalism in some respects was closer to reality than the new cynicism, and that both should be taken with several grains of salt."[11]

Conclusion

Why is it we feel
So little for each other, but for this
That we with nature have no sympathy,
Or with such things as have no power to hold
Articulate language . . .
Say not you love a roasted fowl
But you may love a screaming owl.

The first human beings who emerged on earth inherited a magnificent environment, and they appreciated this fact. However, their appreciation (or better, their reverential awe) was clouded by fear. Events in nature, especially animals, were themselves deified. Civilization has stripped, in a commendable way, human beings of this fear of nature, and of the deification of animals. But it has also stripped human beings of their sense of "the inexhaustible beauty and glory of the web of life" (BS; 228). Paradoxically, it is only now that beauty and glory, in their planetary totality, are "being made accessible by the very industrialism that tends to destroy" them (BS; 229). Our machines have not enabled us to find our place among the natural kinds. Only philosophy and religion can help us do this. The trick is to avoid primitive fear and awe while still respecting animals.

As seen in Chapters One and Two, classical theism's monopolar prejudice led to a conception of God as unmoved by creation, intrinsically unaffectd by animal or even human suffering. Incompatible as this conception was with a belief in a God of love, classical theists modeled their own relationships with animals on it, only this time they "played god" themselves. As a consequence, animals were only respected instrumentally, and their pain did not affect classical theists intrinsically. It should not be surprising that Hartshorne's dipolar conception of God should yield a different conception of animals. If followers of Christ, in particular, are not concerned about all suffering—I know I have made this point earlier—what are they concerned about?

What is needed is a new conception of sainthood (devoid of concern for miracles and the like), a new conception of moral heroism to guide theists in

132

their treatment of animals. Philosophers tend to discriminate, explicitly or implicitly, four types of moral action: (1) some actions are morally neutral, hence they are morally permissible; (2) some actions are morally wrong, hence we ought not to perform them; (3) some actions are duties that we ought to perform; and (4) some actions are above and beyond the call of duty, morally permissible but not morally neutral—these praiseworthy actions are called supererogatory (*erogatio* is Latin for "payment").[1] What sort of actions are vegetarianism and fair treatment of animals? Special attention must be given to vegetarianism because it is a necessary, although not sufficient, condition for any fair treatment of animals. As Peter Singer puts it:

> practically and psychologically it is impossible to be consistent in one's concern for nonhuman animals while continuing to dine on them. If we are prepared to take the life of another being merely in order to satisfy our taste for a particular type of food, then that being is no more than a means to our end. In time we will come to regard pigs cattle, and chickens as things for us to use, no matter how strong our compassion may be.[2]

All will agree that vegetarianism is not morally wrong, so we are left with alternatives (1), (3), and (4). To say that to choose a vegetarian diet over a meat-eating diet is morally neutral decision, like choosing between eating with a fork or a spoon, is to beg the question as to whether or not animals deserve our respect. In fact, those who try to defend or allow meat eating often do so on moral grounds, either explicitly or implicitly. The enormous attention philosophical vegetarianism has received in recent years indicates that not even most opponents to vegetarianism see it as morally neutral. To say that vegetarianism is a morally neutral action is to trivialize it.

We are left with the question: Is vegetarianism (3) or (4)? One might suspect that the status of philosophical vegetarianism would be more exalted if it were supererogatory. But if it is a practice above and beyond the call of duty it would not necessarily have any implications for us who are mere mortals. If one *assumes* that there is no duty to abstain from animal flesh, then philosophical vegetarianism would indeed appear supererogatory. Since most philosophers from the end of the ancient period until rather recently have made this assumption, and this largely because of classical theism, it is not surprising that the received view sees the vegetarian going beyond the call of duty with respect to dietary regimen.

Hartshorne's method often is, along with other supporters of animal rights. to:

identify what seems to be the major outlines of our *considered* moral beliefs, and then to bring logical analysis to bear on these to see whether they square with our apparent *unconsidered* attitude toward the particular matter under investigation (emphasis added).[3]

In the case of our treatment of animals, the contemporary philosophical vegetarian holds that our considered moral belief (or moral truism, as Kai Nielson puts it)[4], that unnecessary suffering should be avoided, does not square with our unconsidered eating of animal flesh, leading many meat-eating philosophers or theologians into a highly casuistical "anthropodicy," a term Stephen R. L. Clark invents to parallel the classical theist's problem with theodicy.[5]

A saintly approach to animals is not necessarily, however, supererogatory. Six possible states of moral character can be imagined, which may help us locate what sort of action vegetarianism is, with the highest sort of moral character first:[6]

(1) Saintly excellence *(arete)*: when one wants to act well, and does so in a saintly way.
   SE1: supererogatory saintliness
   SE2: nonsupererogatory saintliness

(2) Ordinary excellence *(arete)*: when one wants to act well, and does so.

(3) Self-control *(enkrateia)*: when one wants to act badly, but controls oneself.

(4) Lack of self-control *(akrasia)*: when one want to act badly, tries to control oneself, but cannot.

(5) Badness of character *(kakia)*: when one wants to act badly, does so without resistance, thinking it to be good.

(6) Moral ugliness *(aischros)*: a diseased moral character; inhuman.

"To act well" with respect to animals entails, at the very least, if my presentation of Hartshorne is correct, not making them suffer or be killed unnecessarily. In civilized society where vegetal food is abundant, this means that to attain state (2) or (3), one must be a vegetarian. Opponents to vegetarianism exhibit moral character (4), (5), or, in extreme cases of animal torture, (6). Moral character (4) is more prevalent than many suspect. Philosophical vegetarians often hear their colleagues admit that the vegetarian's case is probably right (thereby indicating that vegetarianism is not a morally neutral practice), but nonetheless humorously talk about cows or pigs as they eat their roast beef or ham sandwiches. Nervous laughter usually follows. The existence of moral character (5) probably indicates that there are some basic disagreements about the moral status of animals, the status of rights claims, or some other issue. I hope that a consideration of Hartshorne's thought clear's up at least some of these disagreements.

If one is right in implying that the attainment of states (2) or (3) with respect to animals would require vegetarianism as a duty, then what would saintly excellence (1) consist of? Two sorts of saintliness could be imagined.[7] One could be a saintly vegetarian if one did one's duty (not causing animals to suffer or be killed unnecessarily) regularly in contexts in which desire or some other reason like self-interest would lead most people not to do it even though vegetal food was in abundance (SE2). Or one could be a saintly vegetarian by going above and beyond the call of duty by refusing to make animals suffer or be killed even if it might be deemed "necessary" to do so, in times of drought, etc. (SE1). That is, moral excellence in the form of state (2) or (1) can be attained without supererogation, although (1) can also be, in certain circumstances, supererogatory (as in SE1). Another example of nonsupererogatory saintliness would be the case of a doctor who stayed by his patients in a plague-ridden city when all of his fellow doctors had fled; and supererogation can be seen in the case of a doctor who *volunteered* to go to a plague-ridden city. If the first doctor were interviewed after the plague he might well say, "I only did my (Hippocratic) duty." But only a modesty so excessive as to appear false could make the second doctor say the same. So also, vegetarians in a predominantly meat-eating and affluent culture may be nonsupererogatory saints merely by doing their duty, like the first doctor. To quote Urmson:

> while life in a world without its saints and heroes would be impoverished, it would only be poor and not necessarily brutish or short as when basic duties are neglected. If we are to exact basic duties like debts, and censure failure, such duties must be, in ordinary circumstances, within the capacity of the ordinary man. . . . A line must be drawn between what we can expect and demand from others and what we can merely hope for and receive with gratitude when we get it.[8]

Note that from the perspective of animals raised for the table, life *is* brutish and short because human duties are neglected. The key question seems to be: Is vegetarianism within the capacity of the ordinary person? If not, then the claim that it is a duty would be in danger, because vegetarianism would slip into the category of supererogation, thereby making it largely irrelevant for those who are not moral saints in the sense of supererogatory saintliness (SE1).

The law grants to the general population many things that cannot be granted to the philosopher, theologian, or saint. The general populace can legitimately associate with prostitutes or spend all of their free time in a tavern; it is their right as free agents to do these things. But the legitimacy of civil liberties in the political arena is not always an accurate guide regarding the questions of what we ought to do in the ethical arena. The claim that those things permitted to the multitude cannot be permitted to the philosopher, the theologian, or the saint is not a defense of the supposed ascetic, disembodied character of religious figures. Nor is vegetarianism a type of penance. Denying ourselves what is superfluous is temperance, not penance; the latter only occurs when we deny ourselves what is proper for us to have. Eating is the process by which we can "transubstantiate" vegetal matter into spirit; if we did not eat, we could not pray or think about God. The glutton weighs down prayer and thought with a full belly; analogously, the meat eater fetters them by (unwittingly?) aiding in the infliction of unnecessary suffering and death on animals that recently lowed and cried. Not all of our food turns to dung; some of it is "resurrected" into life, good humor, and, in at least some instances, thought about and commiseration with the sufferings of others, including the sufferings of animals.

Vegetarianism is a duty. (See the arguments from sentiency and marginal cases.) In the present state of culture, however—and this applies to Hartshorne as well—a certain sainthood is required from philosophers and theologians, but more especially from the multitude, in order to meet this duty.[9] This sainthood need not be supererogatory; that is, one only needs non-supererogatory saintliness (SE2) to meet one's duty. Perhaps some day meat eating will go the way of anthropophagy, and speciesism the way of racism and sexism, which no intelligent person defends any longer, in theory at least. If so, we will have to start by refusing to insist on the vast chasm between ourselves and animals that is implied by our eating them. Perhaps then we will be able to begin to appreciate Hartshorne's wisdom. God cares for the fall of *every* sparrow, even if we are of more value than many. Reiterating a theme in his early philosophy from *Beyond Humanism* (1937), Hartshorne has recently stated:

> If we avoid absolutizing man's difference from the rest of nature, we can more easily open our minds and hearts to the really infinite difference, that between any mere animal or mere transitory creature and the Primordial and Everlasting, (FH; 171-172).

Notes

Introduction

1. *The Philosophy of Vegetarianism* (Amherst: University of Massachusetts Press, 1984), also published as *Vegetarianism: The Philosophy Behind the Ethical Diet* (London: Thorsons, 1985), with a Forward by Peter Singer.

2. Abbreviations for Hartshorne's works are listed on p. vii, facing the Introduction.

3. Richard Swinburne is an analytic theist who takes animals into consideration at several points, but he yields classical theistic defects. For example, for Swinburne an omnipotent God sends, or allows, suffering to animals so that others may learn from such suffering. See, for example, his *The Existence of God* (Oxford: Oxford University Press, 1979), pp. 152 ff., 196 ff.

Chapter One

1. It has often been noted that the Old Testament, despite characters such as Deborah, is a sexist document. What is little noticed is that it is equally unfair to animals. A woman and an animal are responsible for the Fall. See Peter Singer, *Animal Liberation* (N.Y.: New York Review, 1975), "Man's Dominion," on which I have relied here in Chapter One.

2. I apologize for calling nonhuman animals just "animals" throughtout this book. It can be a misleading designation. See Mary Midgley, "The Concept of Beastliness," *Philosophy* 48 (1973): 111–135.

3. See St. Augustine, *The Catholic and Manichean Ways of Life*, translated by D. A. Gallagher and L. J. Gallagher (Boston: Catholic University Press, 1966), p. 102. Also see John Passmore, *Man's Responsibility for Nature* (N.Y.: Scribner's, 1974), p. 111.

4. See Passmore, "The Treatment of Animals," *Journal of the History of Ideas*, April-May 1975, p. 196.

5. St. Augustine, p. 91.

6. St. Augustine, *City of God*, I, 20.

7. Homily 29, 471 in *Homilies of St. John Chrysostom on the Epistle of St. Paul to the Romans* (Oxford, 1861).

8. See Passmore, "The Treatment of Animals," p. 198. The prayer goes as follows:

> And for these also, O Lord, the humble beasts who bear with us the heat and burden of the day, we beg thee to extend they great kindness of heart, for thou hast promised to save both man and beast, and great is thy loving kindness, O Master.

Paradoxically, St. Basil may be relying on St. Paul. See Romans 8:19-22:

> The whole creation is eagerly waiting for God . . . . It was not any fault on the part of creation that it was made unable to attain its purpose . . . being freed, like us, from its slavery to decadence, to enjoy the same freedom and glory as the children of God . . . the entire creation . . . has been groaning.

Is groaning?

9. Singer, pp. 215-216. See *St. Francis of Assisi, His Life and Writings as Recorded by His Contemporaries*, translated by L. Sherley Price (London, 1959), p. 145.

10. Dominican Fathers' translation, Third Book, part 2, chapter 112.

11. See Philip Devine, "The Moral Basis of Vegetarianism," *Philosophy* 53 (1978), pp. 502-503.

12. The term seems to have been invented by Richard Ryder, but was popularized by Singer, pp. 9, 27, etc. The term is modeled after the terms "racism" and "sexism."

13. *Summa Theologiae*, IIaIIae, question 64, article 1.

14. Ibid., question 65, article 3.

15. Act IV, scene 2.

16. Stephen R. L. Clark, *The Moral Status of Animals* (Oxford: Clarendon Press, 1977), pp. 110, 191; Andrew Linzey, *Animal Rights: A Christian Assessment of Man's Treatment of Animals* (London: SCM Press, 1976). See also J. Todd Ferrier, *On Behalf of the Creatures* (London: Order of the Cross, 1926).

17. See Singer, pp. 213-214. Also Passmore, "The Treatment of Animals," p. 203.

18. Joseph Rickaby, S. J., *Moral Philosophy* (London, 1892), pp. 248-251 (This text had several editions in the twentieth century.); G. Tyrrell, S. J., "Zoolatry," *Month*, September 1885; and "Jesuit Zoophily: A Reply," *Contenporary Review* November 1885; the latter article is hereafter: Tyrrell. See also Frances Power Cobbe, "The Ethics of Zoophily," *Contemporary Review*, October 1895). Numbers in parentheses in text refer to pages in these latter two sources.

19. On the argument from marginal cases see Singer, p. 265 and Tom Regan, "Fox's Critique of Animal Liberation," *Ethics* 88 (January 1978), pp. 126–133. See also my "Vegetarianism and the Argument from Marginal Cases in Porphyry," *Journal of the History of Ideas* 45 (March 1984), pp. 141-143.

20. Singer, p. 188.

21. See Tyrrell, "Zoolatry". Also see Cobbe, pp. 505-506.

22. See Singer, pp. 171-201. Also James Rachels, "Vegetarianism and 'The Other Weight Problem', " in *World Hunger and Moral Obligation* (Englewood Cliffs, N.J.: Prentice-Hall, 1977).

23. Charles R. Magel, *A Bibliography on Animal Rights and Related Matters* (Washington, D.C.: University Press of America, 1981), especially pp. 151-157 on religion and animals, and pp. 163-186. Also see Lynn T. White, "Christians and Nature," *Pacific Theological Review* 7 (1975), pp. 6-11.

24. Singer, pp. 211-214. Also see Vernon Bourke, *Ethics* (N.Y.: Macmillan, 1951), p. 352 and Austin Fagothy, *Rights and Reason* (St. Louis: Mosby, 1976), p. 197.

25. Published in *Origins* (September 24, 1981), especially p. 221.

26. See Rickaby, p. 152; and Cobbe, p. 504.

27. Henry David Thoreau, *Walden*, ed. J. Lyndon Shanley (Princeton, N.J.: Princeton University Press, 1971), pp. 215-216. Salt was one of Thoreau's first biographers. Cobbe, p. 499, speaks of love for animals as a "higher law," an allusion to Thoreau's "Higher Laws" in *Walden*, where his vegetarian thought is developed. See my *Thoreau the Platonist* (N.Y. and Berne: Peter Lang, 1986).

28. *Thoreau,* pp. 321, 323.

29. Interestingly enough, there is no indication that Adam and Eve had an unfriendly relationship with animals, or ate them, in the Garden of Eden. The ancient Greeks also believed their Golden Age was vegetarian, as Hesiod and others attest. Two other works that develop a sane theological view of creation are Jurgen Moltmann, *God in Creation* (San Francisco: Harper and Row, 1985), and A. R. Peacocke, *Creation and the World of Science* (Oxford: Clarendon Press, 1979).

30. See *The Nation,* August 9, 1906.

31. Louis Berman, *Vegetarianism and the Jewish Tradition* (N.Y.: Ktav, 1982).

32. Rabbi J. David Bleich, "Judaism and Animal Experimentation," in Tom Regan, ed., *Animal Sacrifices: Religious Perspectives on the Use of Animals in Science* (Philadelphia: Temple University Press, 1986), pp. 86, 97 ff.

33. See L. I. Nangeroni and P. D. Kennett, "An Electroencephalographic Study of the Effect of Shechita Slaughter on Cortical Function in Ruminants" (1963), and other studies in Munk, editor, *Shechita* (Jerusalem, 1976).

34. Andrew Linzey, "The Place of Animals in Creation: A Christian View," in Regan, *Animal Sacrifices,* pp. 115-148.

35. Ibid., pp. 116-117. Also see Linzey's "Animals and Moral Theology," in Paterson and Ryder, eds., *Animals' Rights: A Symposium,* (London: Centaur, 1979), as well as an article with the same title by C. E. Turnbull. Linzey's views are opposed to those of John Hick, who views animals merely, it seems, as aesthetic ornamentation used to fill in the gaps in the divine order. See Hick's *Evil and the God of Love* (London: Fontana, 1968), p. 350.

36. James Gaffney, "The Relevance of Animal Experimentation to Roman Catholic Ethical Methodology," in Regan, *Animal Sacrifices,* p. 159.

37. See Al-Hafiz B. A. Masri, "Animal Experimentation: The Muslim Viewpoint," in Regan, *Animal Sacrifices,* pp. 171-198.

38. Narrated by Ibni 'Umar. See the sayings of Muhammed as translated by James Robson (Lahore, Pakistan: Sh. Muhammed Ashraf, 1963), p. 874.

39. See the extremely clear article by Basant Lal, "Hindu Perspectives on the Use of Animals in Science," in Regan, *Animal Sacrifices,* pp. 199-212.

40. Christopher Chapple, "Noninjury to Animals: Jaina and Buddhist Perspectives," in Regan, *Animal Sacrifices,* p. 214.

41. Ibid., p. 228; also pp. 221, 225.

42. Ibid., p. 230. Also see "Animals," in *Encyclopaedia of Buddhism,* edited by G. P. Malalasekara (Ceylon: Government Press, 1965) 4, pp. 667-672; and Philip Kapleau, "Animals and Buddhism," *Zen Bow Newsletter: A Publication of the Zen Center* 5 (Spring 1983), pp. 1-9. Finally, see Jack Austin, "Buddhist Attitudes towards Animal Life," in Paterson and Ryder, pp. 25-33.

43. See F. S. C. Northrup, "Naturalistic Realism and Animate Compassion," in Richard Knowles Morris, ed., *On the Fifth Day: Animal Rights and Human Ethics* (Washington, D.C.: Acropolis Books, 1978), pp. 173-204. Also see Steven Rosen, *Food for the Spirit: Vegetarianism and the World Religions* (N.Y.: Bala, 1987).

44. See Rodney Taylor, "Of Animals and Man: The Confucian Perspective," in Regan, *Animal Sacrifices,* p. 241.

45. Ibid., p. 251. Quoted in James Legge, *The Four Books* (Shanghai: Chinese Book Co., 1930), p. 744.

46. *Walden,* p. 219.

Chapter Two

1. Colin E. Gunton, *Becoming and Being: The Doctrine of God in Charles Hartshorne and Karl Barth* (Oxford: Oxford University Press, 1980), especially pp. 11-55.

2. I will be relying on several of Hartshorne's works prior to 1970 in this chapter; see the bibliography.

3. For Hartshorne, God must be as great as possible at any particular time or else God would not be the greatest conceivable being. But new moments bring with them new possibilities for greatness, which God must realize in the best way possible if God is the greatest or, better, the unsurpassable. This means that God is greater than any being that is not God, but God can always surpass itself. It does *not* mean that God's earlier existence was inferior, because it was at that earlier time the greatest conceivable existence, the greatest existence logically possible, and greater than any other being.

4. See an excellent article by Leonard Eslick, "Plato as Dipolar Theist," *Process Studies* 12 (1982), pp. 243-251.

5. The focus of this book has forced me to ignore much of the good in Gunton's work: his description of Hartshorne's doctrine on relations is the best I have read, his treatment of the difference between God's abstract pole and our abstract description of God is excellent. Gunton also notices that Hartshorne's thought is not so much anthropomorphic but an "anthropopathism." This point, along with Gunton's noticing that Hartshorne's distinction between concrete entities and aggregate entities goes back as far as his *Man's Vision of God* are both well put.

6. Hartshorne makes it clear in "A Logic of Ultimate Contrasts" (CS) that the two poles of each contrast stand or fall together; if either pole is real, the contrast itself (both poles) is real. Although polarities are ultimate, it does not follow that the two poles are equal in every sense, as I have indicated previously regarding the more inclusive character of *becoming* in contrast to *being*. In this sense, an asymmetry is involved, but this asymmetry is compatible with my treatment of polar equality in Hartshorne's theism. Consider that Hartshorne finds the position of Plotinus (and classical theists) inadequate in that, although it is true that without unity and simplicity there is no sense to be made of plurality, etc., it is *equally* true that without plurality, contrast, and complexity, there is no unity, beauty, et al. Incidentally, in Hartshorne's elaborate table of metaphysical contraries (in CS, written after PS), the active–passive pair is not to be found. Finally, see David Richardson, "Philosophies of Hartshorne and Teilhard de Chardin: Two Sides of the Same Coin?" *Southern Journal of Philosophy* 11 (Fall 1964), pp. 107-115.

7. David Tracy, in *The Analogical Imagination* (N.Y.: Crossroad, 1981), indicates that a genuine theology of ecology must root history in nature, otherwise no righteous anthropocentric indignation over our rape of nature will repair the rupture. The question is, Does any believer still *feel* the world as God's creation? Tracy notes that process theology has a readier route to a theology of ecology than any other, in that it can mediate between humanity and God through philosophical reflection, but that it also can make sense of how God's manifestation can erupt through nature itself, as of old. That is, process thought recovers what is best in the Franciscan-Bonaventure tradition of the natural world as sacrament, also found in Teilhard's process thought. See Tracy, pp. 214-215, 228, 379, 381. Another reason for the superiority of process thought over classical theism is that the latter explains suffering through human or angelic free will such that

suffering is meant to benefit only these beings, making animal suffering unintelligible and gratuitous. See David Ray Griffin, *God, Power, and Evil: A Process Theodicy* (Philadelphia: Westminster, 1976). Also see my forthcoming article, "Must a Perfect Being Be Immutable?," where I criticize several analytic philosophers who are classical theists: Eleonore Stump and Norman Kretzmann, "Eternity," *Journal of Philosophy* 78 (1981), pp. 429-458; and William Mann, "Simplicity and Immutability in God," *International Philosophical Quarterly* 23 (1983), pp. 267-276.

8. In addition to "Peace" in Whitehead's *Adventures of Ideas*, see my "Pacifism and Hartshorne's Dipolar Theism," *Encounter* 48 (1987), pp. 337-350. Two other secondary sources are Robert Kinast, "Non-Violence in a Process Worldview," *Philosophy Today* (Winter 1981); and David Basinger, "Human Coercion: A Fly in the Process Ointment?," *Process Studies* 15 (Fall 1986).

Chapter Three

1. See note 3, below.

2. See the excellent article by Susan Armstrong-Buck, "Whitehead's Metaphysical System as a Foundation for Environmental Ethics," *Environmental Ethics* (Fall 1986), pp. 250–259, on which I have relied heavily in this chapter. Regarding my criticisms of other ethical views, see Peter Singer, *Practical Ethics* (Cambridge: Cambridge University Press, 1979); Tom Regan's *The Case for Animal Rights* (Berkeley: University of California Press, 1983), the most sophisticated defense of animal rights to date. See also Aldo Leopold, *Sand County Almanac* (N.Y.: Oxford University Press, 1949) and Genevieve Lloyd, "Spinoza's Environmental Ethics," *Inquiry* 23 (1980). Also on Spinoza, see my "McFarland, Pantheism, and Panentheism," forthcoming in *History of European Ideas*. Frederick Ferre shows himself to be in the tradition of Leopold by arguing for an "organicist ethic," wherein meat can be eaten, but only in moderation. However, it is unclear why we should be "moderate" in our eating of meat by Ferre's own criteria. Because he admits that we should not cause unnecessary suffering to animals, and that we should produce nutritious food as efficiently as possible so as to feed the world's poor humans, he should defend vegetarianism. Further, because admirably Ferre admits (unlike most meat-eaters) that animals become frightened in the abattoir by the cries of other animals and by the smells of slaughter, it seems he should examine more sympathetically the vegetarian response: Do not kill these animals. Ferre's solution has only the facade of humaneness: Protect the animals from these sounds and smells. But this sneaking up on the animal is at odds with Regan's excellently argued point that animals are subjects-of-a-life, or, to put it in Hartshorne's language, they value their own lives. Ferre uses Whitehead at three points: (1) He notes that for Whitehead what constitutes inherent value is value for itself, in that to be valued by another is extrinsic. But (2) despite the fact that Ferre correctly notes that for Whitehead the role of living organisms is not merely to survive (rocks do this better than we do), but to manifest complex structure and dynamic variety, he does not state that animals do have a complex structure and dynamic variety that is eliminated when they are slaughtered. Whitehead

makes it clear in *The Function of Reason,* the text that Ferre relies on here, that the purpose of animals is not so much to live but to live well and live better. (3) Ferre claims to follow Whitehead in not "drawing a line" between animals that are persons and those that are not. But it is clear by Whitehead's criteria, treated elsewhere in this book, that all of the animals raised for the table do have a personal line of inheritance. See Frederick Ferre, "Moderation, Morals, and Meat," *Inquiry* 29 (1987), pp. 391-406.

3. See Karl Popper and J. C. Eccles, *The Self and Its Brain* (Berlin: Springer Verlag, 1977), p. 438, although Popper would not like the word "panpsychism" used to describe his position. See also J. Z. Young, *Programmes of the Brain* (Oxford: Oxford University Press, 1978), p. 19. And see David Bohm, "The Implicate Order: A New Order for Physics," *Process Studies* 8 (1978), pp. 73-102; and Charles Birch and John B. Cobb, *The Liberation of Life* (Cambridge: Cambridge University Press, 1981), pp. 132, 151, 187.

4. See Karl Popper, "Of Clouds and Clocks," in *Objective Knowledge: An Evolutionary Approach* (Oxford: Oxford University Press, 1972). It should be noticed that in the history of philosophy Hartshorne may be the first consistent defender of epistemological realism and metaphysical idealism *together.* As subjects we know real things, but the things we know are always subjects. Also, it is interesting to note that Leibniz's theory of monads was affected by his corresponsdence with Leeuwenhoek, the inventor of the microscope.

5. See Plato's *Phaedrus* and Book Ten of the *Laws,* as well as Chapter Seven of this book. Also see Susan B. Armstrong, *The Rights of Nonhuman Beings: A Whiteheadian Study* (Ph.D. dissertation, Bryn Mawr College, 1976); and John B. Bennett, "Ecology and Philosophy: Whitehead's Contribution," *Journal of Thought* 10 (1975), pp. 24-30.

6. See Hartshorne's "Why Psychicalism: Comments on Keeling's and Shepherd's Criticisms," *Process Studies* 6 (1976), pp. 67-72. Also see two articles by Thomas Nagel in *Mortal Questions* (Cambridge: Cambridge University Press, 1979), "What Is It Like to Be a Bat?", and "Panpsychism."

7. See Robert Neville, "Buddhism and Process Philosophy," in *Buddhism and American Thinkers,* edited by Inada and Jacobson (Albany: State University of New York Press, 1984), pp. 131, 136. In the same volume, see Hartshorne's "Toward a Buddhisto-Christian Religion," pp. 5, 12.

8. See Whitehead's *Adventures of Ideas* (N.Y.: Free Press, 1933), "The Grouping of Occasions." Also see "The Categoreal Scheme" and "The Order of Nature," in *Process and Reality,* corrected edition (N.Y.: Free Press, 1979). Also see Hartshorne, WP, pp. 4, 16, 30, 57, 119-120, 132-133, 148, 175-176, 190, 198. Hartshorne is especially helpful in suggesting that the "specious present" of a human being is probably longer than that of birds, with their higher bodily temperatures, and shorter than that of fish. In this work Hartshorne also condemns Cartesian speciesism.

9. See Whitehead's *Modes of Thought* (N.Y.: Free Press, 1968), p. 151.

10. Armstrong-Buck, pp. 248-249.

11. *Modes of Thought,* p. 4.

12. Erazim Kohák rightly notices that, in response to nature, we must avoid both the callousness of utility *and* the paralysis of sentimentality. See *The Embers and the Stars: A Philosophical Inquiry into the Moral Sense of Nature* (Chicago: University of Chicago Press, 1984), p. 99. Also see Hartshorne's "Biology and the Spiritual View of the World: A Comment on Birch's Paper," *Christian Scholar* 37 (September 1954), pp. 408-409; and "Man in Nature," *Experience, Existence, and the Good,* edited by Irwin Lieb (Carbondale: Southern Illinois University Press, 1961), pp. 89-99. Finally, see Hartshorne's "The Unity of Man and the Unity of Nature," *Emory University Quarterly* 11 (October 1955), pp. 129-141.

Chapter Four

1. See Peter Singer; and Bernard Rollin, "Beasts and Men: The Scope of Moral Concern," *Modern Schoolman* 55 (1978), pp. 241-260.

2. See James Collins, *The Thomistic Philosophy of the Angels* (Washington, D.C.: Catholic University Press, 1947).

3. Ibid., where it is made clear that for St. Thomas angels could not make metaphysical error because they were *imago Dei,* perfect mirrors of divine truth.

4. See Birch and Cobb, *The Liberation of Life,* for some detailed discussion of debates in contemporary ethology. Also, for a suggestion as to how to reconcile animal rights and "deep ecology," see Michael Fox, "Panentheism," *Creation* (July-August 1986), pp. 16-17.

5. Based on Immanual Kant, *Lectures on Ethics,* translated by Louis Infield (N.Y.: Harper and Row, 1963), pp. 239-240. See my review of Christina Hoff's "Kant's Invidious Humanism," in *Ethics & Animals* 4 (September 1983), pp. 93-95. As will be seen later in this paragraph, Kant gives both too much credit to human beings and too little to God and animals.

6. See Vincent Potter, *Charles S. Peirce: On Norms and Ideals* (Amherst: University of Massachusetts Press, 1967), pp. 130-131.

7. See my "St. Augustine, Abortion, and *Libido Crudelis,"* forthcoming in *Journal of the History of Ideas.*

Chapter Five

1. Again, see my *The Philosophy of Vegetarianism.*

2. It should be noted that the word "necessary" in the argument from sentiency is hardly the problem some think it to be, unless, of course, one says that it is necessary to eat meat to satisfy the "demands" of taste, etc. But I suspect that it would be the opponent to the argument who equivocates on "necessary" at this point. Also, on Jesus' remark regarding the fall of a sparrow see Birch and Cobb, *The Liberation of Life,* p. 147.

3. See Stephen R. L. Clark, *The Nature of the Beast: Are Animals Moral?* (Oxford: Oxford University Press, 1982).

4. An alphabetical list of those ancient thinkers of the West who were vegetarian or for whom there is at least some evidence they were vegetarian, would be at least this large: Apollonius of Tyana, Aratus, Aristophon, Crates, Dicaerchus, Diogenes the Cynic, Empedocles, Epicurus, Heraclides, Heraclitus, Hierocles, Iamblichus, Menedemus, Metrocles, Metrodorus, Mnesimachus, Musonius, Ovid, Philodemus, Phoclydes, Plato, Plotinus, Plutarch, Polystratus, Porphyry, Posidonius of Apameia, Proclus, Pythagoras, Seneca, Sextius, Sotion, Theophrastus, Zeno the Stoic. Notice later in this chapter that my claim that Hartshorne ought to defend vegetarianism on the basis of his own principles is analogous to what Theophrastus did for Aristotle.

5. Peter Singer, *Animal Liberation*, p. 188.

6. See John B. Cobb, "Beyond Anthropocentrism in Ethics and Religion," in *On the Fifth Day: Animal Rights and Human Ethics,* edited by Richard Knowles Morris (Washington, D.C.: Acropolis Books, 1978).

7. Again, see James Rachels, "Vegetarianism and 'The Other Weight Problem'. "

8. See G. Simpson, "How Many Species?" *Evolution* 6 (1952), pp. 342-343.

9. See Birch and Cobb, p. 187.

10. Ibid., pp. 153-160. For Hartshorne, see FH; 162, 167, 170; RS; 49, 51, 54, 56, 58; IO; 224. That there are no significant differences between Hartshorne and Cobb can be seen in the former's review of the latter's book, *Is It Too Late? A Theology of Ecology.* See "Cobb's Theology of Ecology," in *John Cobb's Theology in Process,* edited by Griffin and Altizer (Philadelphia: Westminster Press, 1977), pp. 112-115. Here Hartshorne makes it clear that we live in a culture where concern about pollution is a necessary condition for concern about nature (and God), and that any such abusive pollution that rests on the "Christian" exaltation of humanity as the sole valuable form of life is opposed both by an intelligent reading of Darwin and by process metaphysics, where humanity is viewed as the supreme—but not sole—contributor to this planet. But Hartshorne offers no criticisms of Cobb's view of animals.

11. In addition to Singer's *Animal Liberation,* see his *Animal Factories* (N.Y.: Crown, 1980).

12. See the case of "Optical Distortion, Inc.," in Tom Beauchamp, *Case Studies in Business, Society, and Ethics* (Englewood Cliffs, N.J.: Prentice-Hall, 1983). I should also note that John Cobb is no relation, as far as I know, to Frances Power Cobbe, treated in Chapter One. The same is true for Peter Singer and Isaac Bashevis Singer; the latter was mentioned in Chapter Two.

Chapter Six

1. See Alexander Cappon's two studies: *About Wordsworth and Whitehead* (N.Y.: Philosophical Library, 1982); and *Aspects of Wordsworth and Whitehead* (N.Y.:

Philosophical Library, 1983). Also see Keith Gould, "Panentheism in *The Prelude,*" in *Aeolian Harps,* edited by Fricke (Bowling Green, Ohio: Bowling Green University Press, 1976), pp. 111-131.

2. See Jay McDaniel, "Physical Matter as Creative and Sentient," *Process Studies* 5 (1983), pp. 291-317. I have used McDaniel's fine article rather freely in this chapter.

3. All Wordsworth quotations are taken, unless otherwise noted, from Thomas Hutchinson and Ernest DeSelincourt, editors, *Wordsworth: Poetical Works* (Oxford: Oxford University Press, 1974). All word emphasis in Wordsworth's poems are added.

4. See Melvin Rader, *Wordsworth: A Philosophical Approach* (Oxford: Clarendon Press, 1967). Rader quotes Wordsworth as holding that poetry is "the breath and finer spirit of all knowledge; it is the impassioned expression which is in the countenance of all science" (p. 107). Wordsworth's view of the world, compatible with contemporary science, is, according to Rader, most compatible philosophically with the perspectival realism of Whitehead (pp. 186, 192). Further, as Rader rightly holds, Wordsworth's religiosity is not so much pantheism as Hartshornian panentheism, that is, God is not in nature but nature is in God. See my article, "Wordsworth's Panentheism," *The Wordsworth Circle* 16 (Summer 1985), pp. 136-142, for a brief history of scholarship on Wordsworth's panentheism.

5. Some classical theists have come close to suggesting that soul includes body and not vice versa; for example, James Collins is instructive on how an angel occupies a place "virtually" through its "effective operation." Also, for an interesting treatment of how a Nobel-prize-winning scientist may support the idea of a Wold Soul, see J. E. Lovelock, *Gaia: A New Look at Life on Earth* (Oxford: Oxford University Press, 1979) exploring a new—or perhaps revives an ancient—concept of the relationship between the earth and its biosphere. His thesis is that the entire range of living matter on the earth, from whales to viruses and from oaks to algae, can be regarded as a single living entity. This is an alternative to the view of our planet as demented and purposeless, albeit Gaia for Lovelock does not encompass the whole universe and is elaborated (strangely enough) through a cybernetic model.

6. *Ecclesiastical Sonnets,* "Deplorable His Lot," 11 (published 1835). For this quotation see *Prelude* III, 117-121.

7. "Tintern Abbey," 93-102.

8. *Prelude* XIV, 453-454.

9. Ibid. XIII, 276-278.

10. Rader often quotes these lines from *The Prelude* (pp. 36, 198, etc.); see Ernest DeSelincourt, ed., *The Prelude,* 1st ed. (Oxford: Clarendon Press, 1926), p. 512. Also see *Prelude* VIII, 835, where Wordsworth refers to "soul," which "passing through all Nature rests *with* God." I should make it clear that I am dealing specifically with Wordsworth's concept of God in this chapter, not with his attitude toward organized religions, popular pretensions to piety, or the like. Regarding these latter, Wordsworth's thought did change, as is evidenced in his poem "Decay of Piety" (published in 1827).

I am willing to admit a change of emphasis *within* Wordsworth's panentheism as he got older. On all beings existing *in* one mighty whole, see Jonathan Wordsworth, *William Wordsworth: The Borders of Vision* (Oxford: Oxford University Press, 1982), p. 219.

11. Rader, p. 198. In fact pantheism prevents an understanding of the ordinary animal case (OO; 123).

12. *Miscellaneous Sonnets*, "It Is a Beauteous Evening," 6-8 (written 1802). For Plato's crying child, see *Sophist* (249D).

13. *Poems of the Imagination*, "Yes, It Was the Mountain Echo," 19-20 (written 1806).

14. *Excursion* IV, 1141, 1144 (written 1802–1812).

15. *Memorials on a Tour of the Continent* (1820), "The Last Supper," 3.

16. Ibid., "Suggested on a Sabbath Morning," 54.

17. *Prelude* VI, 636-640.

18. *Miscellaneous Sonnets*, "Those Words Were Uttered," 12 (published 1807).

19. *Memorials on a Tour in Italy* (1837), "Eternal Lord," 1.

20. *Miscellaneous Sonnets*, "No Mortal Object," 9-10 (published 1807).

21. Ibid., "The Prayers I Made," 8 (written 1805).

22. *Excursion* IV, 50-51.

23. *Ecclesiastical Sonnets*, "Not Utterly Unworthy," 1 (written 1821).

24. Ibid., "Outstretching Flameward," 2 (written 1821).

25. Ibid., "By Chain Yet Stronger," 8 (published 1827).

26. Ibid., "Scattering Like Birds," 14 (written 1821).

27. *Ode to Duty*, 1-2 (written 1805).

28. *Poems of Sentiment and Reflection*, "The Force of Prayer," 65-68 (written 1807).

29. David Newsome, *Two Classes of Men: Platonism and English Romantic Thought* (London: John Murray, 1974), p. 9.

30. Ibid.

31. See both Rader's and Newsome's books for the sources of Wordsworth's erudition.

32. See Rader, pp. 72-73. Also Newsome, pp. 26-27.

33. G. M. Harper, *The Neoplatonism of William Blake* (Chapel Hill: University of North Carolina Press, 1961), p. 264. Also, Jonathan Wordsworth rightly notices that although Wordsworth got his regulative ideas from Aristotle and Kant, his constitutive ideas came from Plato and Plotinus (but not Spinoza). See his pp. 184, 219.

34. See my *Plato's Philosophy of History* (Washington, D.C.: University Press of America, 1981) on the *Sophist.*

35. Leonard Eslick, "Plato as Dipolar Theist," and "The Dyadic Character of Being," *Modern Schoolman* 21 (1953–1954), pp. 11-18.

36. Eslick, "Plato as Dipolar Theist," p. 245.

37. In addition to Eslick, see the study by P. E. More, *The Religion of Plato* (Princeton, N.J.: Princeton University Press, 1921).

38. Eslick, "Plato as Dipolar Theist," p. 245.

39. On the relationship between Plato's World Soul and Wordsworth's, "One Life," see Jonathan Wordsworth, pp. 39, 74, and 419 note 36. Rader, p. 78, resists the contention that Plato's World Soul is to be identified with deity. See *Timaeus* where it is quite clear that World Soul is a blessed God (34B), and the World Soul is described as perfect (30-31); in the *Philebus,* the World Soul is fairest and most precious (30); also see the *Laws* (896-899) and my "McFarland, Pantheism, and Panentheism."

40. *Metaphysics* A.

41. *Ecclesiastical Sonnets,* "Latitudinarianism" (written 1821). Jonathan Wordsworth, p. 355, asks "Can one usefully blame a man who is searching for the one and the invisible, if he fails to make distinctions?" My response: yes, but Wordsworth *did* make more appropriate distinctions than many realize, even though he always believed in an immanent God. Cf., his p. 180.

42. Jonathan Wordsworth, p. 361, quotes Coleridge as follows: "Deep thinking is attainable only by a man of deep feeling." Hartshorne's aestheticism is compatible with this claim. Finally, those interested in Wordsworth's view of animals should consider "Peter Bell" carefully.

Chapter Seven

1. A fuller treatment of the relationship between "Hartshorne and Plato" can be found in my article with this title, forthcoming in *The Philosophy of Charles Hartshorne* in the Library of Living Philosophers series. There the relationship of Hartshorne's thought to Whitehead's "eternal objects" is treated, as well as the scholarship on Plato that Hartshorne has read, Hartshorne's treatment of the arguments for God in Plato, the theme of dipolarity in Plato and Hartshorne, etc.

2. See J. Prescott Johnson, "The Ontological Argument in Plato," *The Personalist* 44 (1963), pp. 24-34. Also see AD; 139-141, 148-149, 307. Hartshorne also treats Plato's argument from order, which is blended with the cosmological argument (NT; 125; PS; 25; IO; 35-36, etc.).

3. Nonetheless, the Greeks were aware of the nerves. See Friedrich Solmsen, "Greek Philosophy and the Discovery of the Nerves," *Museum Helveticum* 18 (1961),

pp. 150-167, 169-197. Also see my unpublished "Plotinus's Finger in the World-Soul," where I mention Plutarch's claim that all of the ancient philosophers, except for Aristotle and the atomists, believed that the cosmos as a whole was besouled, that is, was a divine animal. Even if Plutarch's claim is an exaggeration, it nonetheless shows hows important this belief was for the ancients.

4. To be included in the divine life (or better, to make a contribution to the divine life) forevermore is enough immortality for Hartshorne, thus putting him somewhat at odds with Plato's arguments in favor of personal immortality (OO; 43; CS; 45). Further, Hartshorne thinks that, in Plato's theory of immortality, Plato was not thinking as a metaphysician, but as a legislator, in that he assumed that providence would offer an extension of our earthly codes (NT; 107).

5. See A. Boyce Gibson, "The Two Strands in Natural Theology," in *Process and Divinity: The Hartshorne Festschrift* (LaSalle, Ill.: Open Court, 1964), p. 422.

6. See my "McFarland, Pantheism, and Panentheism," if this claim seems unsupported.

7. For a fine treatment of Kant's Platonism, see Thomas McFarland, *Coleridge and the Pantheist Tradition* (Oxford: Clarendon Press, 1969).

8. Karl Popper, *The Open Society and Its Enemies* (Princeton, N.J.: Princeton University Press, 1962) 2, pp. 247-250, on the connection between irrationalism and collectivism. For Hartshorne (WM; 45), Plato recognized the problem of democracy (how to get the majority to want the wise to rule), even if he did not solve it.

9. See William Sessions, "Hartshorne's Early Philosophy," in *Two Process Philosophers,* ed. Lewis Ford (Tallahassee, Florida: American Academy of Religion, 1973), pp. 10-34.

Chapter Eight

1. W. H. Thorpe, *Purpose in a World of Chance: A Biologist's View* (Oxford: Oxford University Press, 1978), p. 51. Thorpe relies on the work of Joan Hall-Craggs. On Whitehead's interpretation of Aesop, see Alexander Cappon, *Aspects of Wordsworth and Whitehead,* p. 45.

2. See E. Gavin Reeve, "Speciesism and Equality," *Philosophy* 53 (October 1978), pp. 562-563.

3. Also see Hartshorne's "Metaphysics Contributes to Ornithology," *Theoria to Theory* 13 (1979), pp. 127-140, and "Freedom, Individuality, and Beauty in Nature," *Snowy Egret* 24 (Autumn 1960), pp. 5-14.

4. Kohák, pp. 124-125.

5. Also see R. G. Collingwood, *The Idea of History* (N.Y.: Oxford University Press, 1956), p. 227, where Collingwood suggests that the beginnings of historical understanding are also found in cats, who teach their young about the past.

6. Although birds are not so developed as to need religion, they are sophisticated enough to realize that the farther a song needs to be heard, the more distinctive it needs to be (OO; 90). Hartshorne contrasts his position on animal freedom and educability with that of the last ornithologist who refused to accept evolution, Bernard Altum (1824–1900). Although Altum gave a "splendid account of the territorial theory of bird song" (OO; 88), he assumed that divine providence led to the complete exclusion of randomness in nature, the denial of animal intelligence, and the denial of animals having purposes. Hartshorne sees no problem, however, in a divine ordering in a statistical way of partly free and self-ordering individuals. Altum's adherence to the classical idea of strictly sufficient reason not only leaves no leeway for decision making in animals, it also produces the "nastiest form of the theological problem of evil" (OO; 89).

7. See Santiago Sia, *God in Process Thought: A Study in Charles Hartshorne's Concept of God* (Dordrecht, the Netherlands: D. Reidel, 1985), pp. 11, 39, 46, 96, 117.

8. Thomas McFarland, *Romanticism and the Forms of Ruin* (Princeton, N.J.: Princeton University Press, 1981).

9. See Hartshorne's "Why Study Birds?," *Virginia Quarterly Review* 46 (Winter 1970), pp. 133-140.

10. See Hartshorne's "The Aesthetics of Birdsong," *The Journal of Aesthetics and Art Criticism* 26 (1968), pp. 311-315. The remainder of this chapter relies on that essay.

11. Ibid., pp. 314-315.

Conclusion

1. I am relying to a large extent on two articles by J. O. Urmson; "Saints and Heroes," in *Essays in Moral Philosophy*, ed. A. I. Melden (Seattle: University of Washington Press, 1958) and "Aristotle's Doctrine of the Mean," in *Essays in Aristotle's Ethics*, ed. Amelie Oksenberg Rorty (Berkeley and Los Angeles: University of California Press, 1980). Obviously category (4) is the most controversial, but because I do not place vegetarianism in this category, no harm will be done by examining it. It should be noted that I will use "moral" and "ethical" as synonyms here, and not in the precise senses that Hartshorne sometimes uses. However, I will be making distinctions that are compatible with Hartshorne's uses of these terms.

2. See Peter Singer, pp. 172-173 and 160-163.

3. Jan Narveson, "Animal Rights," *Canadian Journal of Philosophy* 7 (March 1977), p. 164.

4. Kai Nielson, "Persons, Morals and the Animal Kingdom," *Man and World* 11 (1978), p. 233.

5. Stephen R. L. Clark, p. 59. Also see Steven Rosen, *Food for the Spirit: Vegetarianism and the World Religions* (N.Y.: Bala Books, 1987) as well as Richard Schwartz, *Judaism and Vegetarianism* (N.Y.: Exposition Press, 1982), M. I. A. Khalik,

An Article on Islam and Vegetarianism (Madras: The Vegetarian Way, 1977) and Swaren Singh Sanehi, *Vegetarianism in Sikhism* (Madras: The Vegetarian Way, 1977).

6. This list is loosely based on Urmson's "Aristotle's Doctrine of the Mean," p. 58. The fact that we are using Aristotle for the purpose of defending vegetarianism should not bother us because, as Theophrastus shows, Aristotle may have been an inadequate interpreter of his own theories on animals; again, see my *The Philosophy of Vegetarianism*.

7. I am compressing Urmson's three types of sainthood into two. It should also be noted that for Urmson we cannot distinguish state (2) from (3) either by one's actions or beliefs, but only by one's desires.

8. Urmson, "Saints and Heroes," pp. 211, 213.

9. Let me repeat that although Hartshorne never gives an explicit argument for vegetarianism, he often intimates the strengths he sees in the position. (See FH; 162, 167, 170; RS; 49, 51, 54, 56, 58; IO; 224.) Nonetheless, for Hartshorne the greatest evil human beings could do to animal species is habitat destruction. "In this way we take *everything* from them." That is, individual animals are killed as well as the species-dependent mode of enjoyment.

Bibliography

On the relationship between religion and animals see the excellent bibliography of Charles R. Magel, *A Bibliography on Animal Rights and Related Matters* (Washington, D.C.: University Press of America, 1981), pp. 5-6, 151-157. For Hartshorne's works on birds, see *Process Studies* 6 (Spring 1976), pp. 92-93 and 11 (Summer 1981), pp. 147-150. See my *The Philosophy of Vegetarianism* for a lengthy annotated bibliography of articles and books on the philosophy of animal rights and related matters.

On Hartshorne's philosophical works, see, in chronological order:

1. *Beyond Humanism* (Lincoln: University of Nebraska Press, 1968), originally published in 1937. (BH)

2. *Man's Vision of God* (N.Y.: Harper and Brothers, 1941). (MV)

3. *The Divine Relativity* (New Haven, Conn.: Yale University Press, 1948). (DR)

4. *Reality as Social Process* (Boston: Beacon Press, 1953). (RP)

5. *Philosophers Speak of God* (Chicago: University of Chicago Press, 1953). (PS)

6. "Biology and the Spiritual View of the World: A Comment on Birch's Paper," *Christian Scholar* 37 (September 1954), pp. 408-409.

7. "The Unity of Man and the Unity of Nature," *Emory University Quarterly* 11 (October 1955), pp. 129-141.

8. "Freedom, Individuality, and Beauty in Nature," *Snowy Egret* 24 (Autumn 1960), pp. 5-14.

9. "Man in Nature," in *Experience, Existence, and the Good,* edited by Irwin Lieb (Carbondale: Southern Illinois University Press, 1961), pp. 89-99.

10. *Anselm's Discovery* (LaSalle, Ill.: Open Court, 1967). (AD)

11. *A Natural Theology for Our Time* (LaSalle, Ill.: Open Court, 1967). (NT)

12. "The Aesthetics of Birdsong," *The Journal of Aesthetics and Art Criticism* 26 (1968), pp. 311-315.

13. *Creative Synthesis and Philosophic Method* (LaSalle, Ill.: Open Court; and London: SCM Press, 1970). A new edition has been published: (Lanham, Md.: University Press of America, 1983). (CS)

14. "Why Study Birds?" *Virginia Quarterly Review* 46 (Winter 1970), pp. 133-140.

15. "Can Man Transcend His Animality?" *Monist* 55 (1971), pp. 208-217. (CM)

16. *Whitehead's Philosophy* (Lincoln: University of Nebraska Press, 1972). (WP)

17. *Born to Sing* (Bloomington: Indiana University Press, 1973). (BS)

18. "The Environmental Results of Technology," in *Philosophy and Environmental Crisis,* edited by William T. Blackstone (Athens: University of Georgia Press, 1974), pp. 69-78. (ER)

19. "Mysticism and Rationalistic Metaphysics," *Monist* 59 (1976), pp. 463-469. (MR)

20. *Aquinas to Whitehead* (Milwaukee: Marquette University Press, 1976). (AW)

21. "Why Psychicalism: Comments on Keeling's and Shepherd's Criticisms," *Process Studies* 6 (1976), pp. 67-72.

22. "Cobb's Theology of Ecology," in *John Cobb's Theology in Process,* edited by Griffin and Altizer (Philadelphia: Westminster Press, 1977), pp. 112-115.

23. "Foundations for a Humane Ethics: What Human Beings Have in Common with Other Higher Animals," in *On the Fifth Day: Animal Rights and Human Ethics,* edited by Richard Knowles Morris (Washington, D.C.: Acropolis Press, 1978). (FH)

24. *Mind in Nature,* edited by John B. Cobb and David Griffin (Washington, D.C.; University Press of America, 1978). (MN)

25. "The Individual Is a Society," in *The Individual and Society,* edited by Jones, Nobo, Nobo, and Chang (Norman: University of Oklahoma Press, 1978). (IS)

26. "God and Nature," *Anticipation* 25 (1979), pp. 58-64. (GN)

27. "The Rights of the Subhuman World," *Environmental Ethics* 1 (1979), pp. 49-60. (RS)

28. "Metaphysics Contributes to Ornithology," *Theoria to Theory* 13 (1979), pp. 127-140.

29. "In Defense of Wordsworth's View of Nature," *Philosophy and Literature* 4 (1980), pp. 80-91. (DW)

30. "The Ethics of Contributionism," in *Responsibilities to Future Generations: Environmental Ethics,* edited by Ernest Partridge (Buffalo, N.Y.: Prometheus Books, 1981), pp. 103-107. (EC)

31. *Whitehead's View of Reality* (N.Y.: Pilgrim Press, 1981). (WV)

32. Review of Daniel Dombrowski, *Plato's Philosophy of History,* in *Process Studies* 12 (1982), pp. 201-202.

33. *Insights and Oversights of Great Thinkers* (Albany: State University of New York Press, 1983). (IO)

34. *Omnipotence and Other Theological Mistakes* (Albany: State University of New York Press, 1984). (OO)

35. *Creativity in American Philosophy* (Albany: State University of New York Press, 1984). (CA)

36. *Existence and Actuality: Conversations with Charles Hartshorne* (Chicago: University of Chicago Press, 1984). (EA)

37. "God and the Meaning of Life," in *On Nature,* edited by Leroy Rouner (Notre Dame, Ind.: University of Notre Dame Press, 1984).

38. "Toward a Buddhisto-Christian Religion," in *Buddhism and American Thinkers,* edited by Inada and Jacobson (Albany: State University of New York Press, 1984).

39. *Wisdom as Moderation* (Albany: State University of New York Press, 1987). (WM)

My own work on topics related to this book includes, in chronological order:

1. "Rorty on Pre-Linguistic Awareness in Pigs," *Ethics & Animals* 4 (March 1983), pp. 2-5.

2. "Eating and Spiritual Exercises: Food for Thought from Saint Ignatius and Nikos Kazantzakis," *Christianity and Literature* 34 (Summer 1983), pp. 25-32.

3. Review of Christina Hoff, "Kant's Invidious Humanism," in *Ethics & Animals* 4 (September 1983), pp. 93-95.

4. *The Philosophy of Vegetarianism* (Amherst: University of Massachusetts Press, 1984); also *Vegetarianism: The Philosophy behind the Ethical Diet* (London: Thorsons, 1985), with a Forward by Peter Singer.

5. "Vegetarianism and the Argument from Marginal Cases in Porphyry," *Journal of the History of Ideas* 45 (March 1984), pp. 141-143.

6. "Was Plato a Vegetarian?," *Apeiron* 18 (June 1984), pp. 1-9.

7. "A Dialogue on Philosophical Vegetarianism," with Randolph Feezell in *APA Newsletter on Teaching Philosophy* (Late Autumn 1984), pp. 8-10.

8. Review of Charles Hartshorne, *Omnipotence and Other Theological Mistakes,* in *Teaching Philosophy* 7 (October 1984), pp. 358-359.

9. "Wordsworth's Panentheism," *The Wordsworth Circle* 16 (Summer 1985), pp. 136-142.

10. "The Jesuits and the Zoophilists, Again," *The Irish Theological Quarterly* 51 (1985), pp. 232-241.

11. "Polar Equality in Dipolar Theism," *The Modern Schoolman* 62 (May 1985), pp. 305-316.

12. "Thoreau, Sainthood, and Vegetarianism," *The American Transcendental Quarterly* 60 (June 1986), pp. 25-36.

13. Review of Erazim Kohák, *The Embers and the Stars: A Philosophical Inquiry into the Moral Sense of Nature,* in *The Thomist* 50 (July 1986), pp. 481–482.

14. Review of J. K. Anderson, *Hunting in the Ancient World,* in *The Classical Bulletin* 62 (Summer 1986), pp. 51-52.

15. Review of Santiago Sia, *God in Process Thought: A Study in Charles Hartshorne's Concept of God,* in *Religious Education* 81 (Fall 1986), pp. 659-660.

16. "The Ancient Mariner, God, and Animals," *Between the Species,* 2 (Summer 1986), pp. 111-115.

17. "Pacifism and Hartshorne's Dipolar Theism," *Encounter,* 48 (August 1987), pp. 337-350.

18. "Does God Have a Body?," forthcoming in *The Journal of Speculative Philosophy.*

19. "Porphyry and Vegetarianism," forthcoming in *Aufsteig und Niedergang der Romischer Welt* (University of Tübingen).

20. Review of R. G. Frey, *Rights, Killing, and Suffering: Moral Vegetarianism and Applied Ethics,* forthcoming in *International Studies in Philosophy.*

21. "Hartshorne and Plato," forthcoming in *The Philosophy of Charles Hartshorne* (Library of Living Philosophers Series).

22. "Individuals, Species, Ecosystems: A Hartshornian View," forthcoming in *Between the Species.*

23. "McFarland, Pantheism, and Panentheism," forthcoming in *History of European Ideas.*

24. "Two Vegetarian Puns at *Republic* 372," unpublished.

25. "Plotinus's Finger in the World-Soul," unpublished.

26. "Must a Perfect Being Be Immutable?," unpublished.

Index